Home from Home

A guidance and resource pack for the welcome and inclusion of refugee children and families in school

Save the Children UK is a member of the International Save the Children Alliance, the world's leading independent children's rights organisation, with members in 30 countries and operational programmes in more than 100.

Save the Children works with children and their communities to provide practical assistance and, by influencing policy and public opinion, bring about positive change for children.

Salusbury WORLD, set up in 1999, is the only refugee centre in the country based in a primary school. The project provides educational, social and emotional support for refugee children by offering additional English tuition and after-school/holiday activities. It also supports parents and the wider refugee community by providing comprehensive advice and home-school liaison services, family workshops and outings.

Salusbury WORLD serves as a model for other schools with refugee children, and provides guidance and training for a variety of educational professionals.

Published by

Salusbury WORLD   and   Save the Children
Refugee Centre   1 St John's Lane
Salusbury Primary School   London EC1M 4AR
Salusbury Road   UK
London NW6 6RG
UK

First published 2004
Reprinted with corrections 2005

© Salusbury WORLD and The Save the Children Fund 2004

Salusbury WORLD registered charity number 1071065
Save the Children registered charity number 213890

ISBN 1 84187 083 8

Designed by Neil Adams, Grasshopper Design Company
Cover design: Save the Children
Printed by The Redgate Press Limited, UK

Contents

Section 2: Developing play opportunities (51)

Section 3: Involving refugee parents (89)

Section 4: Providing advice and support to parents 107

Bibliography 158

About the authors

Bill Bolloten (Editor) is a freelance consultant on refugee education. Bill has worked as a teacher in Bradford and London and was previously joint co-ordinator of the Newham Refugee Education Team. He has written and published a number of papers and articles, produced educational resources for schools and delivered training to teachers and other service providers. Bill is the moderator of *refed* (refugee education), a national email discussion and mailing list for teachers and other professionals working with refugee children and their families.

Helen Chauncy has taught in primary, secondary and special schools. She has also delivered family literacy and social skills courses.

Nina Chohda managed Salusbury WORLD Refugee Centre from March 1999 to May 2003, taking the project from its inception through to the employment of six staff and the delivery of five main services. Nina managed the centre, the staff, the budget, the fundraising and the general development of the project. She also worked as an adviser on the various social problems experienced by the parents. Nina has a background in working for human rights organisations, photojournalism and teaching English, and is currently completing an MSc in Development Studies. She left the project to pursue a career in emergency relief and development, related to refugee issues internationally.

Johanna Freudenberg was a parent at Salusbury Primary School for the 17 years her children were in the school. She works as a garden designer and artist. The daughter of refugee parents, she values using the teaching of arts and crafts as a means of celebrating a multicultural community.

Joanne Harris is an experienced primary school teacher, having taught in several London boroughs. She has lately specialised in teaching English as an Additional Language (EAL). Joanne has taught EAL at Salusbury WORLD for three years, and supported staff in teaching refugee issues.

Lynne Knight has taught for many years in primary schools in London, specialising in Special Educational Needs, EAL and World Studies. She is currently training teachers and other educational professionals about refugee issues and in adapting their practices to support refugee children and their families.

Jess Mitchell is Salusbury WORLD's Home–School Liaison Worker. She has daily experience of supporting newly-arrived children settle into school and of the issues facing refugee families within the community. She also has experience of running parental workshops and delivering training on refugee issues to teachers.

Hannah Newth has worked as a secondary school teacher in England and Africa. She has experience in campaigning for charities, and has run a range of support services for refugee children aged 8–18 with Asylum Welcome. Hannah joined Salusbury WORLD as a trainer, designing and delivering a practical training package for use with schools and other professionals. She is currently running a befriending project for unaccompanied refugees with Save the Children.

Ben Smith has been at Salusbury WORLD for over two years as an assistant to the project manager and as co-ordinator of Children's Play Opportunities. He also works in an advisory capacity, providing practical assistance to parents and families in the local community. His background is in youth/play work and childcare.

Training for schools and education professionals is provided by:

Salusbury WORLD
www.salusburyworld.org.uk
Tel: 020 7372 2244
Email: mail@salusburyworld.org.uk

Bill Bolloten and Tim Spafford
www.refugeeeducation.co.uk
Tel: 07790 031189
Email: billboll@ntlworld.com

Forewords

Save the Children is an international children's rights organisation committed to making the world a better place for children. Save the Children UK is a member of the International Save the Children Alliance, which has members in 30 countries and operational programmes in more than 100. Save the Children's founder, Eglantyne Jebb, established the first Children's Right Charter and later this formed the basis of the UN Convention on the Rights of the Child which every country in the world, bar two, has signed up to.

Refugee and asylum-seeking children are especially vulnerable and at risk of having their rights denied. These children will have had traumatic experiences in their home countries, have suffered difficult journeys to the UK and continue to suffer while in this county. Many will face racism and discrimination, live in limbo whilst waiting for a decision on their asylum claim and face loneliness and isolation.

In the current environment of anti asylum media coverage and stricter and stricter asylum legislation, Save the Children has prioritised working with refugee and asylum-seeking children in our England programme.

The main objectives of our refugee work are to:
- gather evidence on the impact of asylum legislation on refugee and asylum-seeking children
- use this evidence to inform policy development work with central and local government
- learn directly from refugee and asylum-seeking children to identify and disseminate good practice
- support refugee and asylum-seeking children to undertake self advocacy and raise awareness.

It is within this context that Save the Children is particularly committed to working in partnership with innovative projects like Salusbury World. With their daily contact of providing support and help to refugee children and their families, alongside those within the more settled local community, they help to provide the evidence that develops good practice.

Salusbury WORLD worked with us in producing *In Safe Hands*, a training and resource manual for primary teachers. Over the years London schools have developed much good practice on how best to support refugee and asylum-seeking children. With the dispersal of families throughout the UK, others can benefit from their knowledge.

Home from Home builds on this work and provides very practical guidance to all those who want to provide support and help to this vulnerable group of children and their families.

We are very pleased to share in the work of Salusbury WORLD by helping to support its training and the dissemination of good practice.

John Errington
England Programme Director
Save the Children

Personal experience influences us all. My memory of being physically sick every day before attending a secondary school I hated was arrested only by my father changing his job and our moving to another school in a different part of the country. Once there it was as though the sun had come out. I was made welcome by staff who smiled amid a range of inclusive school practices.

What might it be like for children and their families who come from a different culture and a different country where they have abandoned friends, families and the real and virtual, albeit modest wealth that comes from a stable background suddenly made so unsuitable that they've moved continents to find somewhere safer to live?

Yet these are the experiences of children and their families as refugees and asylum-seekers in our busy capital city. How a school and its LEA welcomes those families and children will make not just an immediate but often a lasting impact on their belief in themselves and in the end the role they feel they can play in our society.

That's why I welcome this book. It shows the way schools and others can play their part in accepting people as they are, knowing their culture and helping them realise their potential to their personal and in the end our collective benefit.

Tim Brighouse
Commissioner for London Schools

Acknowledgements

We would like to thank the following individuals and organisations for their help and support in the writing of *Home from Home*:

- The children and parents from Salusbury Primary School, who have been unstinting in their support, and for their permission to use photographs
- The staff of Salusbury Primary School and Salusbury WORLD, past and present, whose dedicated work forms the basis of these materials
- The volunteers at Salusbury WORLD
- The Trustees of Salusbury WORLD
- Nicky Road of Save the Children
- Victoria McNally of Brent Community Law Centre
- Leila Miller, Nina Chohda, Ben Smith and Johanna Freudenberg for their photographs
- The funders specific to this part of the project: Association of London Governments (ALG), Save the Children Fund
- Tim Brighouse, Commissioner for London Schools and visiting professor at the Institute of Education at London University
- The various professionals who have shared their expertise and work with us along the way.

We are grateful to the following for their critical reading, and further advice and suggestions: Dr Angela Burnett of the Sanctuary Practice, Sara Green of the Royal Borough of Kensington and Chelsea, Val Johnson of MMI-Consultants, Sue Lukes, Shawn Mach of the London Advice Services Alliance, John Grainger of ContinYou, Sanja Potnar of Education Action International/ RETAS, Steve Symonds of Asylum Aid, and Tim Spafford, refugee education consultant.

We have tried by all means possible to contact those who have taken or appeared in any of the photographs we have used. If we have inadvertently left anyone out, we apologise.

Introduction

Introduction

There are over 17 million refugees in the world – roughly one out of every 350 persons on Earth.[1] The vast majority of the world's refugees and other displaced people are cared for in the developing world, especially in Africa, South and Central Asia and the Middle East. Western European countries, the United States, Canada, and Australia shelter less than 15 per cent of the world's refugee population between them. In 2002, the UK ranked 8th in the European Union (EU) for the number of refugees it accepted in relation to its population size.[2]

In the UK, many local education authorities now have refugee[3] children attending their schools. Most of the UK's refugee children attend London schools. Almost one child in 19 in London is a refugee, that is, six per cent of the children in London. However, because of the policy of dispersing asylum-seekers, increasing numbers of refugee children are now attending schools in regions across Britain.

Refugee children arriving in the UK may have experienced loss, danger, upheaval, fear and family separation. They face many challenges: a new language, loss of identity, racism, and poverty. Refugee parents[4] and children also face enormous uncertainties over the outcome of their asylum claim and their future.

Furthermore, in recent years immigration and asylum issues have been the focus of intense media coverage. The negative, exclusionary language and the xenophobia of sections of the British press, particularly the tabloid newspapers, have impacted on the safety of refugee children and young people and created a climate of racism.

Some newspapers have attacked the presence of refugee children in schools and have sought to blame them for 'poor behaviour' and 'disruption'.[5]

School plays a vital role in assisting the recovery and supporting the well-being of refugee children. For refugee children, going to school can help restore normal daily routines and provide a sense of hope and security. School can help refugee children make sense of their experiences, provide them with friends and adults they can trust, and play a central role in helping them regain their self-esteem and confidence.

For schools hosting refugee children for the first time there may be new challenges. Refugee children may arrive at various times during the school year and may be moved on after a short time. They will have diverse backgrounds and needs, including being new to schooling in the UK and needing to learn English. Refugee families may also have complex wider needs related to immigration, housing and health that can impact on children's well-being and progress.

Despite additional demands that may be placed on staff, schools are increasingly remarking on the how the presence of refugee children has had a positive impact on the school community and enriched the learning environment. Refugee children and their parents usually have high expectations of school. Parents are supportive of schools and their children can be highly motivated to learn and make progress.

Welcoming and including refugee children and families

1 Welcoming and including refugee children and families

> "When I came to the UK in January 2001 for asylum, it was like going to the moon for me; strange and unfamiliar. I got dizzy, and I thought that I never can cope with my new life. I was worried about my son and his education and his problem with the new language. He was five years old, and he and I just knew 'hello' and 'goodbye' in English."
>
> **Fatema, parent from Iran**

Setting the context

Like other new children, refugee children will need to feel safe and welcome, and have the support they need to settle in and become effective learners.

Many refugee children are likely to arrive in school after planned admission times, which presents schools with particular challenges. Schools need to plan their work with these new arrivals to ensure good communication with parents, address pastoral and educational needs and promote genuine inclusion. Experience shows that practice which identifies and meets the needs of vulnerable and socially-excluded pupils, including refugee children, can support the development of good practice that helps all pupils.

Ofsted recognises that while high pupil mobility may put pressure on school resources, many schools have developed effective strategies to welcome refugee pupils and help them settle quickly and successfully.

"(Many schools have)… responded positively to the arrival of the asylum-seeker pupils and their families… Dealing effectively with the admission and integration of the pupils had been a steep learning curve, particularly in adapting to their linguistic, cultural and educational needs. Many schools invested considerable time, effort and money… to ensure that the pupils' experience was positive and affirming. There were some remarkable examples of headteachers and staff working extremely hard to ensure that their school adopted a truly inclusive approach to pupils and their parents."
The Education of Asylum-seeker Pupils,
Ofsted 2003

Ofsted's guidance for schools *Evaluating Educational Inclusion* (2000) sets out what it means to be an inclusive school and gives advice on the welcome and induction of new arrivals.

School inspections are now required to evaluate *"how effectively the school inducts new pupils and ensures the needs of particular pupils are being met, for example, by supporting refugee children and recognising the effect of their education being interrupted"*.

Schools must also monitor the extent to which parents from all communities are included by being provided with *"good quality information about the school"*. Inspections will evaluate action taken by a school to *"provide translations of school letters and documents"* and *"draw in parents who may find it difficult to approach school"*.

Many schools are developing effective support for new arrivals by appointing a member of staff to co-ordinate their welcome and admission. At Salusbury Primary School, this has involved the appointment of a Home–School Liaison Worker. Other schools have developed the roles of teachers, teaching assistants and learning mentors, or made links with organisations such as **School–Home Support** and **School Home Liaison** which place trained and experienced home–school liaison workers in schools.

See page 39 for more information on organisations and resources for developing effective home–school liaison.

Welcoming refugee children and families to school

For new arrivals to feel welcome and secure, the whole school environment should be one that values other cultures. Schools should celebrate the diversity of their local communities and the different life experiences, skills, languages and cultures that children bring.

Schools can gain a good understanding of the backgrounds and needs of refugee children if their initial welcome is properly planned and resourced. Below are some strategies for welcome and inclusion.

PLANNING FOR ADDITIONAL ADMISSIONS

An inclusive admissions process is one that welcomes and meets the needs of all children arriving during the year. Being well prepared and having clear procedures will enable time and resources to be used effectively. Good practice to welcome refugee children can improve the inclusion of all new arrivals.

Salusbury Primary School

Salusbury Primary School experiences high levels of pupil mobility. Children joining the school are a diverse group and include many refugees. The school has a clear ethos and commitment to inclusion and entitlement.

According to Headteacher Carol Munro: *"Every child has a right to a good education and this is even more important for children who move on after a short time. In 1999, for example, 300 children joined or left our school at times other than the norm. Each class at Salusbury in every year group receives and says goodbye to children constantly."*

The school has a fluctuating number of refugee pupils on the roll, but they generally make up around 15 per cent of the school population.

The school builds links with the families of refugee children to ensure that their needs are addressed holistically. Refugee parents are often coping with considerable stresses and pressure. The school has learned that parents will take an active part in school life and in their children's learning if they receive support with their wider needs.

Salusbury WORLD has developed a post of **Home–School Liaison Worker** to co-ordinate the welcome, admission and induction of refugee pupils.

The Home–School Liaison Worker:

- welcomes new refugee pupils and their families and provides information on the school system and curriculum in English and home languages

- ensures teachers and other relevant staff are informed about the background, previous educational experience and needs of refugee pupils

- promotes class and peer welcome strategies

- monitors how children are settling in

- contributes to the development of whole-school policies and procedures for welcoming and supporting refugee children

- facilitates home–school communication and makes sure parents have information about their child's progress

- provides family learning workshops in school

- builds up a register of parents who may be able to help in school

- liaises with other agencies and services to ensure parents get appropriate advice and support.

DEVELOPING CLEAR ADMISSION AND INDUCTION PROCEDURES

Many schools have found it helpful to identify the key aspects of the admission process and the roles that different members of staff will play. It is most important that the following information is clearly set out:

- how to record information on a child and family and sensitively gauge their wider needs
- which members of staff will welcome and interview children and families
- which days of the week welcome interviews will take place
- arrangements for providing interpreting if required
- arrangements for providing a tour of the school
- which day(s) of the week new arrivals will start
- which staff will help families apply for free school meals, if appropriate
- the role of Ethnic Minority Achievement teachers and other staff

- which staff will initially assess language and learning needs
- how information from the interview and any initial assessment will be disseminated to class teachers and other key staff, including the SENCO if appropriate.

See the **School admission form checklist** on page 25 for a list of what to include on an admission form.

PROVIDING PARENTS WITH INFORMATION ON THE SCHOOL

Many schools now provide translations of letters and welcome booklets. Welcome booklets provide essential information for parents – eg, start and finish times, the curriculum, uniform requirements and free school meals (see page 27 for suggested contents of the welcome pack). Schools may wish to collaborate in producing translations and share the cost.

CREATING MULTILINGUAL/MULTICULTURAL DISPLAYS

Multilingual displays, resources and other materials around the school and welcome posters in the school entrance can help to promote diversity and make refugee families feel welcome.

Mantralingua (see page 105) produces a wide range of multilingual posters and other materials for schools.

ADMISSION INTERVIEWS

It is good practice to have an initial admission interview with all children and families. It is particularly helpful for refugee families who may be unfamiliar with how schools work in the UK. Schools will need to sensitively gather information

about children's previous educational experiences and develop an understanding of their needs. An admission interview provides an opportunity to create trust between parents and teachers and a successful home–school partnership.

An admission interview should take place a few days before the child starts school, so that information can be conveyed to help the teacher and the class prepare for the new pupil's arrival.

Schools should take the time to review their existing admission practice and consider what features can be built on and what aspects may be difficult and unhelpful for families. Many refugees may have been through several interviews both at home and in this country which may have been intrusive and stressful.

If parents don't speak English, schools should provide interpreters. If an interpreter has been arranged, more time will be needed for the

interview. See **Guidelines for using interpreters** on page 26.

An admission interview can:
- develop an awareness of a family's current situation and identify any issues that may affect a child's well-being
- provide parents with translated information about the school
- help the family to fill in the admission form and apply for free school meals and school clothing grants
- provide parents with a welcome pack containing information about the school and the local area. See page 27 for suggestions of what to include in a welcome pack for parents
- refer families to agencies where they can seek advice and support for wider needs. See pages 139–156 for information on organisations and services that give advice to families.

"When I first came, I didn't speak English. It's not easy. You just have to look and listen, but can't talk. My uncle helped me. That's why I had to go to college to learn English. You can't get someone to help you every day. Now I really like to help translate for the others whenever I can."

Deka, parent from Somalia

Using volunteer interpreters at Salusbury WORLD

At Salusbury Primary School there are many parents who speak different languages and are also proficient in English. Because of the contact we have with families, at the induction interview and through other services we provide, we have been able to recruit a pool of volunteer interpreters.

We keep and update a list of interpreters for each of the main languages who can be called on to support the school. Parents are initially asked if they would like to bring their own interpreter – if they don't, or are not in a position to, then we will call on one of our volunteers.

Volunteer parent interpreters may be asked to interpret over the telephone if there is an emergency, or more commonly, to come into school for meetings such as parent/teacher conferences. We have found that many parents welcome the opportunity to support each other and contribute to the school in this way.

Volunteer interpreters are provided with initial training that covers issues such as confidentiality.

SUPPORTING SCHOOL ADMIN STAFF

First impressions can make a big difference to visitors to a school. School admin staff have a key role to play in welcoming families and they should be included in any training provided on refugee children.

> At Salusbury WORLD, the Home–School Liaison Worker works alongside administrative staff to raise awareness of the needs of children and assist them in identifying those pupils who are likely to be refugees.

See **Identifying refugee and asylum-seeking pupils** on page 28 for guidance on how schools can identify refugee and asylum-seeking pupils, and also the **Language/country of origin checklist** on page 29, which contains an up-to-date list of countries from which refugees are likely to come, along with a list of languages they are likely to speak.

DEVELOPING A POLICY FOR REFUGEE CHILDREN

Following the introduction of the Race Relations (Amendment) Act 2000, all schools are required to have a policy for race equality which clearly states that it covers members of all ethnic groups represented in the school community, including refugees.

Some schools with significant numbers of refugee pupils have developed a specific policy for refugee children that links to the main race equality policy. The **School policy on refugee children** on page 33 is an example from Salusbury Primary School of a school policy on refugee children.

PREPARING FOR NEW ARRIVALS IN THE CLASSROOM

Children of all ages often show tremendous goodwill in welcoming new arrivals. Teachers can draw on this resourcefulness to help refugee children settle and make progress.

It is essential that teachers are given adequate notice of the arrival of a new child, as well as relevant background and educational information, in order to plan effective classroom welcome activities. Teachers should be aware that many refugee children report experiences of racism

> "The host children are central to the 'solution'… All children must be encouraged to contribute to the creation of a supportive and welcoming environment. The arrival of new children provides opportunities for children of all ages to learn about empathy, sharing and caring, respect and kindness. Teaching against racism and stereotyping can help to develop positive attitudes."
>
> *Relearning to Learn: Advice to teachers new to teaching children from refugee and asylum-seeking families*, **National Union of Teachers, 2002**

and prejudice in school. Schools have a responsibility to challenge racism and must have clear procedures for dealing with racist incidents. Promoting an awareness of the experiences of refugee children in the curriculum, for example through Circle Time, can develop empathy and understanding.

Refugee Week, an annual event in June, can provide a focus for schools to learn about refugees and celebrate their contributions to life in this country. During Refugee Week, schools organise activities, displays and assemblies. Some schools collaborate with artists, theatre groups and writers and put on special events for children and parents. This is a good time to involve parents in school activities. More information about Refugee Week can be found at www.refugeeweek.org.uk.

Information for learning about refugees, including Circle Time sessions, can be found on pages 44–45.

"My mum said I had to go to another school because I was bullied. I hoped I didn't have to go through what I had. I went to Salusbury school. When Mrs Sullivan asked who would look after me, lots of people put up their hand. I felt better."

Mariam, 11, from Somalia

Classroom welcome strategies include:
- **ensuring that teachers, other staff and pupils pronounce a child's name correctly**
- **preparing the classroom environment for new arrivals.** Teachers should:
  - have a coat peg labelled with the child's name
  - have a chair and desk space ready
  - have books labelled with their name
  - have a 'buddy' identified (see below)
  - provide materials appropriate for children at the early stages of acquiring English as an additional language (EAL) if necessary
- **providing children with a welcome pack.** At Salusbury Primary School, all new refugee children are provided with a welcome pack that includes:
  - a school book bag
  - a ruler, pencil and rubber
  - a set of colouring pencils
  - a small dual-language word book (*Words for School Use*, published by the Refugee Council)
- **encouraging peer support/buddying.**

Peer support or buddying schemes are an effective way for children to welcome new arrivals to a school. The planning for buddy schemes should actively involve pupils, and should be regularly monitored, evaluated and given a high status in the school. Presenting certificates to buddies in school assemblies will give recognition to the skills and achievements of pupils involved.

Buddies can perform a range of tasks with new arrivals, including:
- reading a 'welcome to our class' book with a new child (see page 37)
- showing the child around the school
- pointing out where things are kept in the class
- helping to explain the work that has to be done
- helping with learning English
- looking after the child at playtime.

Circle Time sessions provide good opportunities to consult and involve pupils in buddying and to develop peer-support skills. It is good practice to allocate buddies to all new children, not just those who are refugees.

It is helpful if a buddy shares the first language of a new arrival, although this is not essential. It is more important that a buddy is responsible and has good social and communication skills.

See **Guide for the Official Class Buddy** on page 35 and the section on peer support on page 41.

WELCOME ACTIVITIES
It might be helpful if new children can get on with some tasks straight away with their buddy.

See **Welcome activities** and **What can you see around the school?** on pages 37–38 for class welcome activities and a sample page of a welcome activity booklet.

Helping refugee children become effective learners

Inclusive schools monitor the progress and achievement of all groups of children. They plan to meet diverse learning needs and ensure that vulnerable or disadvantaged children receive appropriate support.

Schools should evaluate their teaching and learning policies to ensure that refugee children are making progress and achieving their potential. Schools with the best practice for refugee children have encouraged team working and use a range of strategies to create the right environment to motivate individuals and develop their confidence and self-esteem. Good practice for refugee children is good practice for **all** children.

Key aspects of planning for the progress and achievement of refugee children are as follows.

ENSURING EVERY CHILD IS SEEN AS A UNIQUE INDIVIDUAL AND THEIR LANGUAGE, SKILLS, BACKGROUNDS AND EDUCATIONAL EXPERIENCES ARE VALUED

Refugee children will have had diverse experiences of education. They may have attended school in their country of origin, had no previous schooling or experienced a disrupted education. Some children may have attended several schools in the UK. Good admissions procedures will enable the school to record previous learning and identify children's skills, knowledge and interests.

Teachers should be made aware of children's educational histories and build on their previous learning. It helps if records from previous schools in the UK are requested promptly.

HAVING HIGH EXPECTATIONS

Refugee children make good progress in schools where teachers have high expectations and communicate them effectively to children and parents. In these schools, pupils of all ethnic backgrounds and with a range of learning needs are seen as potential high achievers.

ENSURING THAT CHILDREN TAKE A FULL PART IN THE CURRICULUM

When planning curriculum activities, teachers should be aware of the cultural, linguistic and religious diversity in their class and school community, and of the need to develop approaches that include all children. It is vital that refugee children feel part of the normal classroom learning environment and are not further marginalised by having to do large parts of their learning in separate groups working on activities that are unconnected to the mainstream curriculum. Care should be taken to ensure that children's confidence and self-esteem are not affected by working separately.

DEVELOPING AN INCLUSIVE CURRICULUM

Schools can promote refugee children's achievement by ensuring that topics, activities, and learning materials are relevant to their language, religion and culture.

MAKING THE CURRICULUM ACCESSIBLE

Teachers should carefully plan for the EAL needs of refugee children and use a range of strategies to make learning activities accessible across the

"Despite these unimaginable conditions we have appreciated the opportunities which have been offered to us through our primary and secondary schools and have been very grateful to all the people who have supported and believed in us. I hope to achieve my lifetime dream of becoming a doctor. I may not be able to serve this society at present in an influential way but I believe I can contribute my determination, ambitions and hard work to the community and hope that in the future I can make a change, be it small or large."

Ardita, 13, from Albania

curriculum. A variety of approaches have been developed by teachers and Ethnic Minority Achievement teams to support pupils learning EAL. These include:

- **collaborative activities**: these enable children to work in small groups and develop language skills. Collaborative activities are designed to ensure that curriculum-related language is used by children during the activity. Examples include: track games; sorting activities; the 'Fish Game'; true/false activities; barrier games.
- **structured oral work in pairs, small groups and Circle Time**: examples include using sentence starters and scripts that can be orally modelled, extended and scaffolded by other children.
- **opportunities to practice more complex language skills in collaboration with others**: examples include describing, classifying, predicting.
- **frames to scaffold writing in different genres across the curriculum**: these provide children with the start of a sentence around which to base their writing. They can take the form of reports, explanations, a procedure or a recount.
- **Directed Activities Related to Text (DARTS)**: strategies that help learners interact meaningfully with print and make text more manageable to read. They also enable children to develop skills such as skimming, scanning and reading for inference. Group discussion will play a central part. Examples include: filling in missing words or cloze; underlining key words in text; completing a diagram or table using text or other sources as a reference.

- **Visual supports**: examples include Talking Wall – a visual representation of some aspect of a curriculum subject – eg, the stages of a maths or science investigation; key vocabulary cards; representing or organising information diagrammatically, using time lines, grids and Venn diagrams.

Teachers should consider how children are grouped for collaborative activities. Factors to think about include first language, friendships, current abilities, gender and access to supportive peers and good models of English use.

Resources for supporting bilingual pupils are listed on page 46.

ENCOURAGING USE OF FIRST LANGUAGE
Children should be encouraged to use their home language in school. This boosts self-esteem and confidence. Parents may need to be reassured that using home languages supports children's progress in English and their achievement generally in school.

OFFERING ACTIVITIES THAT HELP CHILDREN MANAGE EXPERIENCES OF LOSS AND CHANGE
Most refugee children show great resilience despite the many adversities they have faced. Going to school, making friends and feeling a sense of belonging all support positive coping and mental well-being.

Circle Time, autobiographical and life story activities can also help children understand and express their feelings in a safe environment, provided their language development needs are supported. Creative and group activities such as

music, play, drama, art and storytelling also develop social skills and improve motivation and learning.

Most refugee children will not need specialist mental health interventions or psychotherapy. However, at times, teachers may have ongoing concerns and feel unable to offer the support a child needs. In these cases it is advisable to discuss concerns with the Special Educational Needs Co-ordinator (SENCO) and consider what support is available locally.

In the Midst of the Whirlwind: A manual for helping refugee children (Naomi Richman,

Trentham Books, 1998) provides useful guidance for teachers. Organisations that provide mental health support are listed on page 43.

DEVELOPING FLEXIBLE PROVISION
There is no 'blueprint' or 'one size fits all' approach to ensuring refugee children progress well in school. At times, schools may wish to develop work and projects with small groups of refugee children. Small group work, linked to the curriculum, can introduce collaborative working skills, literacy texts and familiarise children with key vocabulary. A quiet, nurturing environment can also build confidence, self-esteem and trusting relationships with an adult or peers.

MONITORING AND TRACKING PROGRESS

Systems already developed by schools to monitor progress can assist to assess progress being made by refugee children. Schools can use these records to target extra support.

PROVIDING ADDITIONAL SUPPORT

In many schools, teachers and other staff offer additional support programmes – eg, homework, computer and after-school clubs. Schools may need to prioritise refugee children for access to this provision. Section 2 contains advice on setting up after-school play and learning opportunities for children.

PARENTAL INVOLVEMENT

Schools should look at ways that refugee parents can support their children's learning. Section 3 provides a range of ideas on how to do this.

Monitoring refugee children at Salusbury Primary School

At Salusbury Primary School, the progress of all children is monitored. The Salusbury WORLD Home–School Liaison Worker visits classes to check progress of refugee children.

The Home–School Liaison Worker follows up issues that have been raised by class teachers. These have included:

- a child not making expected progress

- a child unable to complete homework tasks

- a child losing weight and not eating in the canteen

- a child with poor attendance

- a child who was tired because of studying late at night.

The Home–School Liaison Worker also informs the class teacher of any circumstances in a family that may affect a child's behaviour and progress in class.

Guidance, photocopiable resources and activities

School admission form checklist

A school admission form should record the following information:

- name and sex of child

- name the child is commonly known by

- child's date and country of birth

- address, and whether this is temporary or permanent accommodation

- home telephone number

- languages spoken and read at home

- languages used for previous education if outside the UK

- whether the parent requires or has requested translation of documents and interpreting at meetings

- position of child in the family

- brothers and sisters

- religion

- dietary requirements

- medical details including name and address of family doctor

- details of parents and carers including country of birth and languages spoken

- emergency contacts

- whether the child has had a recent change of carer

- whether the child is in public care

- entitlement to free school meals (Do parents receive Income Support, Income-Based Jobseeker's Allowance, Child Tax Credit, NASS support or Social Services asylum support?)

- the date a child was first admitted to a UK school

- all previous schools attended (including in any other countries) and any time spent out of school

- early years and pre-school experience

- other educational experience – eg, supplementary school or religious classes

- additional information that the parent wishes the school to know about, including any special educational needs

- identification of a child's ethnicity using the 2001 census categories and agreed local variants

- the expectations of the family and child

- other important information about the child and family.

Guidelines for using interpreters

The use of interpreters should be central to a school's commitment to effective communication with parents who do not speak English. However, finding interpreters is not always easy. Services and resources vary greatly across the UK. Some local education authorities provide interpreting services free to schools; in other areas, schools have to pay for them.

Parents often bring their own interpreter with them to a meeting and may feel more comfortable talking with someone they know rather than a stranger. However, the disadvantages of this are that interpreting may not be accurate and some issues, such as family relationships or child protection concerns, may be difficult to discuss.

Schools should also be aware that they have a duty of confidentiality in respect of parents and the information that they may provide. It may, therefore, be inappropriate to discuss some issues with other family members or friends of parents. Professional interpreters are usually bound by confidentiality agreements and codes of conduct.

Children are sometimes asked to act as interpreters for their parents. However, this may place inappropriate responsibilities on them, particularly where an issue being discussed is not something they would normally be expected to know about.

Sometimes other children in the school are used as interpreters. However, this may disrupt the child's studies, especially if they are called on to help more than once.

When working with an interpreter:

• allow more time for appointments

• spend a few minutes explaining and discussing with the interpreter how each of you will work

• arrange seating in a triangle so that everyone can see each other

• teachers and interpreter should introduce themselves

• explain that both teachers and the interpreter are bound by confidentiality agreements

• maintain eye contact with the parent rather than the interpreter

• address the client directly as 'you' rather than speaking to the interpreter and referring to the person as 'she' or 'he'

• speak slowly and clearly, using straightforward language and only one or two sentences at a time

• ensure that everything you say to the interpreter in front of the parent is interpreted. If you and the interpreter have a private conversation, the parent may feel uncomfortable

• try to have a short conversation with the interpreter after the session. He or she may be able to offer additional feedback on cultural issues.

Adapted from *Meeting the Health Needs of Refugees and Asylum Seekers in the UK*, by Angela Burnett and Yohannes Fassil, NHS, 2000.

Suggested contents of welcome pack for parents

Information about the school

- a copy of the school handbook
- information about school uniform if appropriate
- school term and holiday dates
- school rules
- curriculum information
- Home–School Agreement

Information on getting around the local area

- tube and bus map
- street map of the local area

Adult education and ESOL

- leaflets from the local adult education centre and information on English classes

Health

- NHS Direct telephone service 0845 4647
- list of GPs in the area
- local health advocacy services

Advice

- a list of local organisations providing advice

General information

- sports and leisure facilities, swimming pools, etc
- services such as Sure Start, mother and toddler groups and Children's Fund Projects

Information for refugees and asylum-seekers

- translated information booklets for refugees published by the Refugee Council (www.refugeecouncil.org.uk)

Identifying refugee and asylum-seeking pupils

A **refugee** is person who has fled from his or her home country or is unable to return to it "owing to a well-founded fear of being persecuted for reasons of race, religion, nationality, membership of a particular social group or political opinion". (UN Convention on the Status of Refugees, 1951)

An **asylum-seeker** is a person who has crossed an international border and is seeking safety or protection (ie, seeking recognition as a refugee) in another country. An asylum-seeker is someone who declares her/himself to be a refugee, but whose claim has not yet been determined.

A claim for asylum can be for refugee status under the 1951 Refugee Convention, or for humanitarian protection under the Human Rights Convention. In Britain, asylum-seekers are awaiting a Home Office decision as to whether they can remain here.

Identifying refugee pupils

Effective admissions procedures can help schools identify children who are likely to be refugees. This process of identification, however, should not be a bureaucratic exercise that is intrusive and uncomfortable for parents. It is not necessary for schools to ask to see immigration and asylum documents, nor ask direct questions about immigration status. Schools should avoid asking questions such as: 'Are you a refugee?'

The underlying aim of good admissions practice should be to create an atmosphere of trust and confidentiality where parents and the school can talk and share information. Schools may need to explain to parents why information is recorded, and how it helps the school support their child's progress.

The information that schools will gather for all new entrants is often sufficient for identifying refugee and asylum-seeking children. A child's country of origin, their ethnic background and the language(s) spoken by a family are very good pointers. The language/country of origin checklist that follows may be helpful to schools. It contains an up-to-date list of countries that refugees are coming from, along with a list of languages they are likely to speak. Schools can also find out which groups of refugees are currently coming to the UK to seek asylum. This information can be found on the websites of the Refugee Council www.refugeecouncil.org and the Home Office www.homeoffice.gov.uk.

Language/country of origin checklist

Pupils from the countries, or speaking the languages listed below may be from
a refugee background. However, it should not be an automatic assumption that
all pupils from these backgrounds are refugees or asylum-seekers.

List 1 – by country of origin (likely languages in brackets)

Afghanistan	(Farsi, Pashto, Dari, Tadzhik)	**Ethiopia**	(Amharic, Tigrinya, Oromo, Somali, Sidamo)
Albania	(Albanian)	**Gambia**	(English, Wolof, Mandinka/Malinke)
Algeria	(Berber, Arabic, French)		
Angola	(Portuguese, Umbundu, Kimbundu, Kikongo, Chokwe, Lingala,)	**Georgia**	(Georgian)
		Ghana	(Akan, Twi, Fanti Ga, Ewe, Adangme, Gurma, Dagbane)
Armenia	(Armenian)	**India**	(Hindi, Urdu, Panjabi, Kashmiri, English and others)
Bangladesh	(Bengali, Sylheti)		
Belarus	(Russian, Belarussian)	**Iran**	(Farsi, Azeri, Kurdish, Arabic, Assyrian, Armenian, Turkmen)
Bosnia	(Bosnian, Croatian, Serbian)		
Bulgaria	(Bulgarian, Turkish, Romani)	**Iraq**	(Arabic, Kurdish, Assyrian, Turkmen, Armenian)
Burma	(Burmese, Karen, Shan)		
Burundi	(Rundi, Kinyarwanda, French, Swahili,	**Ivory Coast**	(French)
		Kenya	(Swahili, Luo, Kikuyu, English)
Cameroon	(French, English, Fang, Bulu, Fulani, Mbum, Yaounde, Duala)	**Kosova**	(Albanian, Serbian)
Chad	(French, Arabic)	**Lebanon**	(Arabic, French, Armenian, Kurdish, Assyrian)
China	(Cantonese, Mandarin, Hokkien, Hakka)		
		Liberia	(English, Krio/Americo)
Colombia	(Spanish)	**Latvia**	(Latvian, Russian)
Croatia	(Croatian)	**Lithuania**	(Lithuanian, Russian)
Czech Republic	(Czech, Romani)	**Macedonia**	(Macedonian, Albanian)
Congo (Congo-Brazaville)	(French, Linglala, Kikongo, Teke)	**Moldova**	(Moldovan, Romanian, Russian, Ukrainian, Gaugaz)
DR Congo	(French, Lingala, Kiswahili, Kikongo, Tshiluba)	**Nepal**	(Nepali)
		Nigeria	(English, Yoruba, Ibo, Hausa)
Ecuador	(Spanish, Quechua)	**Pakistan**	(Panjabi, Urdu, Pashto, Kashmiri, Sindhi, English)
Eritrea	(Tigrinya, Tigre, Arabic, Saho, Beja, Afar/Danakil, Baza, Barya, Bilen,)		
		Palestine National Authority	(Arabic)

Poland	(Polish, Romani)
Romania	(Romanian, Hungarian, Boyash, Romani)
Rwanda	(Kinyarwanda, Swahili, French)
Serbia	(Serbian)
Sierra Leone	(English, Krio, Mende, Temne,)
Slovakia	(Slovak, Romani)
Slovenia	(Slovenian)
Somalia	(Somali, Chimiini/Bravanese, Bajuni, Arabic)
Sri Lanka	(Tamil, Sinhala)
Sudan	(Arabic, Nubian, Acholi, Beja, Dinka, Nuer, Shilluk, Zande, Bari, English)
Tanzania	(Swahili)
Turkey	(Turkish, Kurdish,)
Uganda	(English, Luganda, Acholi, Swahili, Nkole, Chige, Gisu, Toro, Nyoro and others)
Ukraine	(Ukrainian, Russian)
Former USSR	(Russian, Azeri, Armenian, Chechen, Georgian, Abkhazian, Lithuanian, Latvian and others)
Vietnam	(Vietnamese, Cantonese, Khmer)
Zimbabwe	(Shona, Ndebele, English)

List 2 – by language (likely country of origin in brackets)

Abkhazian	(Former USSR)
Acholi	(Sudan, Uganda)
Adangme	(Ghana)
Afar/Danakil	(Eritrea)
Amharic	(Ethiopia)
Arabic	(Algeria, Chad, Egypt, Eritrea, Iraq, Lebanon, Palestine National Authority, Somalia, Sudan)
Albanian	(Albania, Kosova, Serbia, Macedonia)
Armenian	(Armenia, Iran, Iraq, Lebanon, Former USSR)
Assyrian	(Iran, Iraq, Lebanon)
Azeri	(Iran, Former USSR)
Bajuni	(Somalia)
Bari	(Sudan)
Barya	(Eritrea)
Baza	(Eritrea)
Beja	(Eritrea, Sudan)
Belarussian	(Belarus)
Bengali	(Bangladesh)
Berber	(Algeria)
Bilen	(Eritrea)
Bosnian	(Bosnia)
Boyash	(Hungarian)
Bravanese/ Chimiini	(Somalia)
Bulgarian	(Bulgaria)
Bulu	(Cameroon)
Burmese/Myan	(Burma)
Cantonese	(Vietnam, China)
Chechen	(Former USSR)
Chige	(Uganda)
Chokwe	(Angola)
Croatian	(Croatia)
Czech	(Czech Republic)
Dagbane	(Ghana)

Danakil	(Eritrea)	Luo	(Kenya)
Dari	(Afghanistan)	Macedonian	(Macedonia)
Dinka	(Sudan)	Mandinka/	
Duala	(Cameroon)	Malinke	(Gambia)
Ewe	(Ghana)	Manderin	(China)
Fang	(Cameroon)	Mbum	(Cameroon)
Fanti	(Ghana)	Mende	(Sierra Leone)
Farsi	(Iran, Afghanistan)	Moldovan	(Moldova)
French	(Algeria, Cameroon, Chad, Congo, DR Congo, Ivory Coast, Lebanon, Rwanda)	Myan/Burmese	(Burma)
		Ndebele	(Zimbabwe)
		Nepali	(Nepal)
Fulani	(Cameroon)	Nkole	(Uganda)
Ga	(Ghana)	Nubian	(Sudan)
Galle	(Ethiopia)	Nuer	(Sudan)
Gaugaz	(Moldova)	Nyoro	(Uganda)
Georgian	(Georgia)	Oromo	(Ethiopia)
Gisu	(Uganda)	Panjabi	(India, Pakistan)
Gurma	(Ghana)	Polish	(Poland)
Hakka	(China)	Portuguese	(Angola)
Hausa	(Nigeria)	Pashto	(Afghanistan, Pakistan)
Hokkien	(China)	Quechua	(Ecuador)
Hindi	(India)	Romani	(Czech Republic, Poland, Romania, Slovakia)
Hungarian	(Hungary, Romania)		
Ibo	(Nigeria)	Romanian	(Romania, Moldovan)
Karen	(Burma)	Rundi	(Burundi)
Kashmiri	(India, Pakistan)	Russian	(Former USSR – including Latvia, Lithuania, Moldova)
Khmer	(Vietnam)		
Kikongo	(Angola, Congo, DR Congo)	Saho	(Eritrea)
Kikuyu	(Kenya)	Serbian	(Serbia, Kosovo)
Kinyarwanda	(Burundi, Rwanda)	Shan	(Burma)
Krio	(Sierra Leone, Liberia)	Shona	(Zimbabwe)
Kurdish	(Kurmanji, Sorani/Zaza dialects – Iran, Iraq, Turkey)	Shilluk	(Sudan)
		Sidamo	(Ethiopia)
Latvian	(Latvia)	Sinhala	(Sri Lanka)
Lingala	(Angola, Congo, DR Congo)	Slovak	(Slovakia)
Lithuanian	(Former USSR)	Slovenian	(Slovenia)
Luganda	(Uganda)	Somali	(Somalia, Ethiopia, Kenya)

Spanish	(Colombia, Ecuador)	**Turkish**	(Turkey, Cyprus)
Swahili	(DR Congo, Kenya, Uganda, Rwanda, Burundi, Tanzania)	**Turkmen**	(Iran, Iraq)
		Twi	(Ghana)
Sylheti	(Bangladesh)	**Ukrainian**	(Ukraine, Russia, Moldova)
Tadzhik	(Afghanistan)	**Umbundu**	(Angola)
Tamil	(Sri Lanka)	**Urdu**	(Pakistan, India)
Teke	(Congo)	**Vietnamese**	(Vietnam)
Temne	(Sierra Leone)	**Wolof**	(Gambia)
Tigre	(Eritrea)	**Yaounde**	(Cameroon)
Tigrinya	(Eritrea, Ethiopia)	**Yoruba**	(Nigeria)
Toro	(Uganda)	**Zande**	(Sudan)
Tshiluba	(DR Congo)		

Reprinted with permission from *Managing Mid-phase Pupil Admissions: A resource and guidance folder for schools*, Newham Education Action Zone (2003)

Salusbury Primary School policy on refugee children

Our philosophy

Refugee pupils are not a homogenous group. They come from many different countries and from different ethnic groups within countries. They have different educational backgrounds; some may not have attended school at all while others may have learned through English in their home countries.

Salusbury Primary School is a multiracial, multicultural, multilingual and multi-religious school. We value this for the diversity of experience and knowledge it brings. We positively encourage both adults who work in the school and the children to respect each others' beliefs, languages, family structures and ways of life. We help children understand the world in which they live and how individuals, groups and nations depend upon each other.

An important element of our philosophy towards refugee children in Salusbury School is our Equal Opportunities Policy on Race. This policy sets guidelines for all members of the school community. It attempts to counter racism through "self-examination; the development of self-worth in all pupils; the curriculum, both formal and hidden, assemblies; home, school and community links".

We welcome the diversity of languages and dialects within our school as they contribute to the richness of school life. We encourage children to be proud of themselves, their languages,

The education of the child shall be directed to the:

- development of the child's personality, talents and mental and physical abilities to their fullest potential
- development of respect for human rights and fundamental freedoms, and for the principles enshrined in the Charter of the United Nations
- development of respect for the child's parents, his or her own cultural identity, language and values, for the national values of the country in which the child is living, the country from which he or she may originate, and for civilisations different from his or her own
- preparation of the child for responsible life in a free society in the spirit of understanding, peace, tolerance, equality of sexes and friendship among all peoples, ethnic, national and religious groups and persons of indigenous origin
- development of respect for the natural environment.

The United Nations Convention on the Rights of the Child, Article 29

backgrounds and traditions. Through the curriculum we share information about the refugee home countries with all pupils.

Our aims

We believe in making all possible efforts to effectively integrate newly-arrived refugee pupils and their families into the school system. We attempt to do this in a number of ways:

The needs of refugee children: All staff in the school are made aware of the particular needs and difficulties faced by refugees. These may include:

- facing loss and mourning
- trauma which can be experienced periodically at irregular intervals after the original trauma
- cultural transition from their home culture to the new country of exile
- the effects of torture or witnessing torture
- lack of knowledge about the well-being of their families or what the future holds
- poor housing
- poverty
- difficulties in accessing mainstream services
- social isolation
- language differences
- encountering prejudice and discrimination.

While teachers may not be qualified to meet these needs, an awareness of them will certainly help them understand the behaviour and development of these children and the need to create a safe and secure environment.

Class teachers recognise the need for the children to be supported in settling into the school. They welcome the children and pair them with others in the class to support their transition and to encourage the whole class to support newcomers. They recognise that sometimes the children need to talk to someone on a one-to-one basis about feelings. This may be the teacher, deputy head, or headteacher. Also because of their experiences, there may be uneven development academically, socially and emotionally and the children may need time to play.

Admissions policy: From the first contact with refugee families we assist them in receiving free meals, school uniform grants and any other financial or material assistance available. We also provide information on the various organisations able to give support.

Translation and interpretation services: We aim to provide translation and interpretation services wherever possible. This may include written and taped abbreviated versions of the school handbook, and translations of the admissions form and other documents. Within the school we have identified pupils and parents willing to interpret on a daily or emergency basis. This is an ongoing process and dependent to a large extent on the willingness of others to give their time.

Guide for the Official

Class Buddy

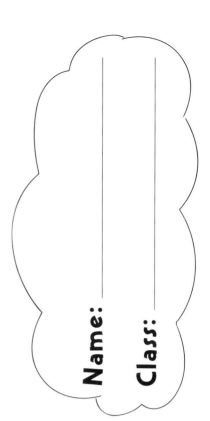

Name: _____

Class: _____

For the first few weeks

Make sure your new friend doesn't get lonely.

Can you speak his/her language? If you can, help translate any words that are difficult. If you can't, introduce her/him to someone else in the class who speaks their language if possible.

Tell your teacher if you think the new pupil is unhappy or finding something difficult.

Thank you!

Thank you offering to help _____ in his/her first few weeks at school.

Welcoming a new pupil to your class is a very important job.

It can be frightening starting a new school, especially if you can't speak English or of you have never been to school in England before. So the new child will need your help and support.

Because you are doing such an important job, you will receive a reward. After your first week as a buddy, come and see us with the new pupil and tell us how you have been helping him/her.

On the first day

1. Introduce yourself to the new pupil and learn his/her name. Explain that you will be looking after him/her.

2. Introduce the new pupil to your teacher and to the class.

3. Help the new pupil to learn important words we use everyday in school. Use the exercise "What can you see around the school" (ask your teacher for a copy).

4. Take the new pupil on a tour of the school. Make sure he/she knows where the canteen and the toilets are in particular.

5. Look after the new pupil during playtime and lunch.

6. Tell him/her about the classroom and playtime rules.

Welcome activities

'What can you see around the school?'

With a digital camera, take photographs of key locations around the school. Prepare vocabulary cards to match each photograph. Ask a buddy to help the new pupil match the picture to the correct word. Encourage them to write the words in their own language if they are able to. The buddy can then take the pupil on a tour of the school to find the places in the photographs (see page 38).

Who's who?

Take photos of some of the key people in the school – eg, the headteacher, school nurse or school secretary.

Ask a buddy to take the pupil around the school finding out who these people are and writing their names next to their photo.

'Welcome to our class' book

Making a 'welcome to our class' book can promote an ethos of welcome and inclusion. It is also a useful and enjoyable ICT or Circle Time activity at the beginning of the school year.

With a digital camera, take a photo of each child in the class and ask them to write a sentence or a short piece about themselves.

Remember to take photos of new pupils when they arrive so they can be added to the book. The book can also be a good way to remember children who may have left over the year.

What can you see around the school?

1. Can you and your buddy match the word to the right picture?

2. Can you write the word in your own language?

3. Ask your buddy to show you these places.

School office	Library	Toilet	Playground

English:

Your language:

English:

Your language:

English:

Your language:

English:

Your language:

Further information and resources

Home–School Liaison

School–Home Support
www.schoolhomesupport.org.uk
Unit 6
Bow Business Exchange
5 Yeo Street
London E3 3QP
Tel: 020 7538 3479

School–Home Support has developed an experienced network of workers to build links between schools and families. Support ranges from one-off interventions to regular home visits, individual work with children to identify and overcome specific barriers to learning, and support to parents in accessing specialist services where necessary.

School Home Liaison (SHL)
Sir John Cass's Foundation CE Primary School
St. James' Passage
Duke's Place
London EC3A 5DE
Tel: 020 7929 3010
Email: schoolhome@btconnect.com

School Home Liaison is a charity that aims to promote partnerships between schools and parents. SHL workers respond to a wide range of needs including attendance, behaviour management, pupils at risk of exclusion, communication with families, improvement of social provision and access to healthcare. They also establish parents' groups such as community language classes, family literacy/numeracy classes and parenting skills sessions. SHL workers are currently working in the London boroughs of Westminster, Camden, Islington and the City of London. They can offer advice to schools elsewhere.

Home School Policies: A practical guide (1995)
by Titus Alexander, John Bastiani and Emma Beresford
£15, ISBN: 0 9526368
Published by Jet Publications, 67 Musters Road, Ruddington, Nottingham NG11 6JB

Also available from the Advisory Centre for Education, 1C Aberdeen Studios, 22 Highbury Grove, London N5 2DQ. Tel: 020 7354 8318
www.ace-ed.org.uk

Parents and home are the biggest influences on children's achievement. This practical guide includes a range of materials to develop policies which improve home school relationships.

Welcoming refugees and other additional admissions

Getting to Know Your School: Information about schools for newly arrived families (2002)
£10 to schools in Liverpool; £15 elsewhere. Available from PSP Working with Bilingual families, Smithdown Primary School, Chatsworth Drive, Liverpool L7 6LJ.

A useful folder which explains schools and the English education system in an attractive and parent-friendly format. Some information is specific to Liverpool, but could be easily adapted.

Information booklet for asylum-seekers with school-age children (2002)
This booklet is aimed at newly arrived asylum-seekers and those giving them advice. It outlines the education system in Manchester, including national curriculum requirements, admissions, nursery/early years provision, ESOL classes, library services and youth services. The booklet is available from Manchester EMAS and can also be downloaded for free in PDF format from: www.manchester.gov.uk/education/emas/

Welcome Booklet CD Rom
£35 + VAT published by Mantra Lingua, Global House, 303 Ballards Lane, London, N12 8NP
wwww.mantralingua.com

This software allows schools to produce a personalised booklet, including key information – such as school rules and opening hours – and photographs of the school, in 18 different languages.

Managing pupil mobility: guidance (2003)
www.standards.dfes.gov.uk/sie/publications/

This DfES publication looks at ways of measuring pupil mobility and at how to develop information systems and analysis. It provides guidance on auditing school provision and examples of good practice, including effective admission procedures and support strategies.

Pathways to learning for new arrivals (2004)
www.qca.org.uk/newarrivals

The QCA has published curriculum guidance to help teachers respond to the needs of pupils newly arrived from overseas. The guidance is designed to promote educational achievement by providing information on best practice and children's rights and entitlements, and includes a series of case studies.

Peer support

Stepping Forward: Working together through peer support (2003)
by Elizabeth Hartley-Brewer
£8.50, ISBN: 1 900990 81 4
Published by NCB Publications
Available from the National Children's Bureau,
www.ncb.org.uk
A summary is available as a free download from:
www.ncb.org.uk/resources/psf_briefing_
stepping.pdf

Stepping Forward clarifies the breadth and scope of peer support, and offers explanations of the different approaches. It provides a number of examples to demonstrate how peer support is being developed in different settings, and offers practical guidance for developing and implementing programmes.

CHIPS – ChildLine in Partnership with Schools
www.childline.org.uk

CHIPS helps schools to set up schemes that encourage pupils to support one another. It gives young people the opportunity to develop practical skills such as communication, listening, understanding and administration.

CHIPS has published a 12-page guide, *Setting Up a Peer Support Scheme*, for teachers and other professionals who wish to set up and assist with peer support schemes. This is available as a download from: www.childline.org.uk/pdfs/
peersupportscheme.pdf

The Peer Support Forum
www.mentalhealth.org.uk/peer/forum.htm

The Peer Support Forum represents over two dozen national voluntary and local organisations which are involved in promoting peer support projects in schools.

Peer Support Manual (2002)
by Jo Scherer-Thompson
£60 (£25 for those working in schools)
ISBN: 1 903645 23 9
Published by Mental Health Foundation and available from their publications department:
Tel: 020 7802 0300 or email: books@mhf.org.uk

A guide to setting up a peer listening project in educational settings.

Resources for Circle Time

Quality Circle Time
www.circle-time.co.uk

Quality Circle Time has been developed by Jenny Mosley over the past 15 years as a whole-school approach to enhancing self-esteem and positive behaviour and relationships within the school community. The website provides advice, information on publications and training, and a selection of free resources.

Quality Circle Time in the Primary Classroom (1996)
by Jenny Mosley
£19.95, ISBN: 1 85503 229 5
Published by LDA Publications

This is an indispensable guide for teachers wanting to get started or needing to build on their Circle Time approach. Revealing the strategies for positive relationships and the steps to create calm and self-disciplined behaviour, the book also includes a range of ready to use Quality Circle Time lesson plans

More Quality Circle Time (1996)
by Jenny Mosley
£19.95, ISBN: 1 85503 270 8
Published by LDA Publications

The follow-up volume facilitates a further journey of evaluating your current Circle Time practice and deepening its effectiveness. Ideas include how to make use of a Quality Circle Time Kitbag, how to adapt ideas for nursery and reception classes, and how to use visualisation and puppets.

Photocopiable Materials (1996)
by Jenny Mosley
£15.95 ISBN: 1 95301 220 4
Published by Positive Press Ltd

This A4 spiral-bound book is packed with designs to use for target charts, forms and notes for specific Circle Time activities (such as Golden Time Choices, Positive Lunchtime Behaviour, Congratulatory Notes), self-esteem exercises and much more. All designs have summary descriptions or instructions to help you quickly put them to good use.

Emotional support and well-being

The Medical Foundation
www.torturecare.org.uk
111 Isledon Road
London N7 7JW
Tel: 020 7697 7777

The Medical Foundation provides survivors of torture in the UK with medical treatment, practical assistance and psychotherapeutic support. The Medical Foundation has a child and adolescent team which helps children and adolescents reach some understanding of their experiences. The team can guide a young person through the difficult process of learning to live in exile and coping with parents who are often changed dramatically by their own experiences of loss and mourning. The Foundation works via music, drawing, painting, dance, mime, drama, poetry and writing stories as a route to helping children to integrate their own painful and positive experiences.

The Place to Be (P2B)
www.theplace2be.org.uk
Wapping Telephone Exchange
Royal Mint Street
London E1 8LQ
Tel: 020 7780 6189
Email: enquries@theplace2be.org.uk

The Place to Be (P2B) is a charity that helps children deal with their emotional reactions to the difficulties they encounter during their school years – divorce, deprivation, abandonment, long-term family illness and death, domestic violence, homelessness, eating disorders, physical or sexual abuse and the trauma of war zone refugees. P2B works with schools across the UK and aims to provide their direct service in 250 schools by 2005, reaching some 75,000 children annually.

Refugee Support Centre
47 South Lambeth Road
London SW8 1RH
Tel: 020 7820 3606

The Refugee Support Centre operates in London and provides free services in counselling and psychotherapy to refugees in their language of choice, activity groups for refugees who are 50+ and living in the borough of Lambeth, Lewisham or Southwark, and family therapy for refugee families or couples.

Nafsiyat Intercultural Therapy Centre
www.nafsiyat.org.uk
262 Holloway Road
London N7 6NE
Tel: 020 7686 8666
Email: enquiries@nafsiyat.org.uk

Nafsiyat provides a psychotherapy service for clients from diverse ethnic and cultural backgrounds based in London.

Learning about refugees

Refugees: A resource book for primary schools (1998)
£4.50, ISBN 0 946787 77 8
Published by the Refugee Council

A popular resource book for 5–11-year-olds containing activities, personal testimonies and background information. Invaluable for teachers wishing to cover refugee issues as part of Citizenship, English, History, Geography, Religious Education and other subjects. Comes with a *Journey to Safety* game.

Kosovan Journeys: Refugee children tell their stories (2001)
£6, ISBN: 0 946787 43 3
Published by the Refugee Council

Two refugee children tell their stories in this colourful A3 book for literacy hour reading and activities.

Why Do They Have to Fight?: Refugee children's stories from Bosnia, Kurdistan, Sri Lanka and Somalia (1998)
£4.50, ISBN: 0 946787 18 2
Published by the Refugee Council

A source book of refugee children's stories and paintings, for Key Stage 2 and 3 Citizenship Studies. Contains basic facts and figures about refugees, a short dictionary of key words and phrases, and a resource list.

A Long Way From Home: Young refugees in Manchester write about their lives (2002)
£2.50, ISBN: 0-9542874-0-1
Published by Ahmed Iqbal Ullah Race Relations Archive and Save the Children

Young refugees in Manchester give accounts of their lives and their experiences as refugees. The book contains stories of fear, anxiety and destruction as well as of relief and happiness. To order a copy, email: rrarchive@man.ac.uk or tel: 0161 275 2920.

Refugees: We left because we had to (2004)
£19.95, ISBN: 0 946787 59 X
Published by the Refugee Council

Comprehensive and authoritative, the third edition of this best-selling book has been completely re-written for the Citizenship curriculum. Jill Rutter sensitively addresses the difficult issue of asylum seekers and refugees. The book is full of ideas and activities that have been tried and tested in the classroom. Each chapter contains photographs, drawings, maps and games to bring the subject alive to students.

Credit to the Nation (2002)
£7.95, ISBN: 0 946787 25 5
Published by the Refugee Council

Refugees have made a massive cultural, social and economic contribution to life in the UK. This recently updated and acclaimed study traces the history of refugee settlement in the UK, and looks at the positive contributions that refugee groups and individuals have made to this country in a changing political and social context.

A Welcome Experience: A PHSE and Citizenship Programme of Work for Key Stages 1 & 2
by Carolyn Herbert
£12.99
Published by Westminster EAZ, School Effectiveness Group, Millbank School Site, Erasmus Street, London SW1P 4HR
Telephone 020 07641 2096

A comprehensive PSHE programme based around the refugee experience, with photocopiable worksheets.

I Am Here: Teaching about refugees, identity, inclusion and the media (2004)
£15.00, ISBN 1 84187 087 0
Published by Save the Children

A citizenship resource pack for 11–14 year olds, including photocopiable activity and information sheets and a video of young refugees talking about their lives.

Educational resources from UNHCR
A range of resources are available from the UNHCR office in London. They include: teachers' guides and films, lesson plans, magazines and booklets, posters and display materials, and videos.

To obtain a full UNHCR educational resource list and to place orders, visit: www.unhcr.org.uk/info/resources/teachtools.html

Global Eye
www.globaleye.org.uk

A useful website for children. The archives contain ideas for learning about refugees.

Other books for children

Home is a Place Called Nowhere (2000)
by Leon Rosselson
ISBN 0 19 271914 9
Published by Oxford University Press

The Colour of Home (2003)
by Mary Hoffman
ISBN 0711219915
Published by Frances Lincoln Ltd

Refugee Boy (2001)
by Benjamin Zephaniah
ISBN 0-7475-5086-7
Published by Bloomsbury

Zlata's Diary: A child's life in Sarajevo (1995)
by Zlata Filipovic
ISBN 0140374639
Published by Puffin Books

The Other Side of Truth (2000)
by Beverley Naidoo
ISBN 0-14-130476-6
Published by Puffin

One Day We Had to Run (2000)
by Sybella Wilkes
ISBN 0237520958
Published by Oxfam Educational

Petar's Song (2004)
by Pratima Mitchell
£5.99, ISBN 0 71122 078 6
Published by Frances Lincoln Ltd

The Breadwinner (2004)
by Deborah Ellis
£4.99, ISBN 0 19275 284 7
Published by Oxford University Press
Parvana's Journey and *Mud City* by the same author complete the trilogy.

Resources for supporting bilingual pupils

Words for School Use (2001)
Published by the Refugee Council
Price: £2.40 each

Albanian and English	ISBN: 0 946787 92 1
Arabic and English	ISBN: 0 946787 37 9
Persian and English	ISBN: 0 946787 42 5
Kurdish Sorani and English	ISBN: 0 946787 58 1
Kurdish, Turkish and English	ISBN: 0 946787 32 8
Somali and English	ISBN: 0 946787 22 0
Serbo-Croat, Bosnian and English	ISBN: 0 946787 58 1

A series of illustrated classroom word lists in languages spoken by refugee children. Targeted at newly arrived children who are just beginning to learn English, they can be also be used for children with little or no literacy in their mother tongue to help them develop reading and writing skills in those languages.

Bilingual Folk Tales

Published by the Refugee Council
Arabic Folk Stories from Algeria & Iraq (1998)
£3, ISBN: 0 926787 62 X
The Adventures of Nakhodak (2001)
(Dari and Afghan Pashto), £3.60,
ISBN: 0 946787 48 4
The Boy with the Empty Pot (1998)
(Bosnia), £3, ISBN: 0 946787 72 7
The Deceiver (1998)
(Somalia), £3, ISBN: 0 946787 57 3

The Leopardess and Her Cubs (1998)
(Democratic Republic of Congo), £3,
ISBN: 0 946787 52 2
The Man Who Understood Animals (1998)
(Albania), £3, ISBN: 0 946787 92 1
The Three Brothers (2001)
(Kurdish Sorani)
£3.60, ISBN: 0 946787 09 3
The Woodcutter (1998)
(Tamil), £3, ISBN: 0 946787 67 0
Sengilo, Mengilo (1998)
(Kurdish), £3, ISBN: 0 946787 13 1

These colourful illustrated books each tell a popular folk tale from a different country, matching the English translation against the tale told in its original language. Suitable for early years and primary schools. Each book carries details of the country where the folk tale originated.

Science Words for School Use (2003)
Published by the Refugee Council
£3.20 each

Arabic and English	ISBN: 0 946787 19 0
Persian and English	ISBN: 0 946787 24 7
Somali and English	ISBN: 0 946787 29 8
Tamil and English	ISBN: 0 946787 34 4

Maths Words for School Use (2003)
Published by the Refugee Council
£3.20 each

Arabic and English	ISBN: 0 946787 39 5
Persian and English	ISBN: 0 946787 44 1
Somali and English	ISBN: 0 946787 49 2
Tamil and English	ISBN: 0 946787 54 9

All About Me: My picture and word book (2003)
£15. Available from Lewisham PDC, Kilmorie Road, London SE23 2SP, Tel: 020 8314 6146

A useful pack of photocopiable materials aimed at newly arrived pupils with little English. It has two parts: 'All about Me' and 'My Picture and Word Book' which the pupil can make into their own dual language picture dictionary. They are divided into topics such as home, school, food, calendar etc.

Language Works: Language and literacy development (1992)
by Robin Shell
£4.99, ISBN 1 873928 79 3
Published by Learning Design

Language Works offers tested strategies for language and literacy development in the multi-lingual classroom. The strategies offered in this book are based on the principles that we learn language as we use it, that we learn through language and that we learn best about language when there is real purpose to the learning. It offers active ways of delivering the National Curriculum for English. The activities it suggests are particularly powerful for bilingual learners because they involve the children actively in their learning.

Language Works 2: Strategies for the multi-lingual classroom (1997)
by Robin Shell
£5.99, ISBN 1 873928 50 5
Published by Learning Design

This book is for teachers who believe that becoming literate is a developmental process which nevertheless needs to be carefully

structured. Following the introduction of the Literacy Hour, *Language Works 2* enables teachers to teach spelling and punctuation in meaningful, purposeful and fun contexts. It offers teachers good ideas on how to extend writing activities into other areas of the curriculum.

Telling Tales: Rewritten literary texts for the multi-lingual classroom (1993)
by Jenny Quintana
£7.50, ISBN 1 873928 64 5
Published by Learning Design

Telling Tales is a resource book for teachers wishing to extend the range of their literature work in the multilingual classroom in Years 6, 7 and 8. It provides ideas for using 12 stories and poems and allows the pupils to practice reading, writing, speaking and listening skills. It contains over 50 illustrated, copyright-free photocopiable worksheets and detailed teachers' notes for using the materials. Based on successful classroom practice both in London and abroad, it is suitable for the entire ability range at Key Stages 2 and 3. The suggested activities are particularly suitable where classes include children who are learning EAL.

Strategies to Support EAL Pupils in Literacy (2001)
£5
Available from: Hounslow Language Service, Hounslow Education Centre, Martindale Road, Hounslow TW4 7HE
Tel: 020 8583 4166/4167
www.ealinhounslow.org.uk

This booklet answers teachers' questions about supporting Key Stage 1 and 2 pupils in the literacy hour, and in literacy development generally.

Challenging Children: An inventory of strategies for busy teachers who want to get the best out of their pupils (2002)
by Annie Dryden and Satpreet Mitchell
£12
Published by EMAS Hackney Edith Cavell Building, Enfield Road, London N1 5BA
Tel: 020 8356 7357

This booklet pulls together various strategies used by teachers to make work across the curriculum accessible to pupils and involve them in a variety of collaborative activities.

Supporting Bilingual Learners in Schools (1996)
by Maggie Gravelle
£14.99, ISBN: 1 85856 053 5
Published by Trentham Books

Bilingualism is an asset and this book describes the approaches and strategies that best support and develop the skills of bilingual learners. Underpinned by a lucid account of the theoretical framework and the research on which it is constructed, this book sets out what should be done in the classroom and why.

Planning for Bilingual Learners: An inclusive curriculum (2000)
Edited by Maggie Gravelle
£14.99, ISBN: 1 85856175 2
Published by Trentham Books

This book offers a framework for teachers to include bilingual learners in their curriculum planning. It considers what is needed for the curriculum to be accessible to all children and provides the necessary framework for action. Experienced teachers show how they have used this framework to plan effectively for bilingual learners in both primary and secondary classrooms and in a range of curriculum areas, so enhancing the learning of all the pupils, whether monolingual English or bilingual/multilingual.

Home Pages: Literacy links for bilingual children (2000)
By Charmian Kenner
£12.99, ISBN: 1 85856 212 0
Published by Trentham Books

Home Pages shows how teachers can build on children's home experiences when they write in the classroom. Based on a year-long research project in a south London nursery class, the book offers practical guidance on creating a multilingual literacy environment in the early years. Ideas include finding out about children's literacy worlds, encouraging families to bring materials in home languages into school and inviting parents to act as readers and writers in the classroom.

Enriching Literacy
Compiled by Robin Richardson for Brent Language Service
£9.99, ISBN: 1 85856 163 9
Published by Trentham Books (1999)

Teachers in Brent Language Service have been examining how children learn to use English as an additional language in their speech and writing in the classroom, and *Enriching Literacy* is the result. It sets out the practical strategies and activities that help bilingual children become competent in the formal academic language the curriculum requires. The book suggests practical classroom activities, keeping to the fore the importance of high cognitive challenge. Appropriate texts are identified and there are checklists to assist with auditing and policy-making, which cover not only specific aspects of language development but also the overall context in which language development in the classroom takes place.

Being Bilingual: A guide for parents, teachers and young people (1995)
by Safder Alladina
£9.99, ISBN 1 85856 051 9
Published by Trentham Books

In *Being Bilingual*, Safder Alladina talks directly to bilingual parents and young people about the role of their home languages and how they can, and should, be developed and maintained.

Websites

Nottingham EMAG
www.nottinghamschools.co.uk/emag

This site has been developed by the Nottingham Citys EMAG service and features a series of EMAG guidance documents giving an overview of EMAG and useful guidance on target setting, recording progress, partnership teaching, etc.

Manchester Ethnic Minority Achievement Service
www.manchester.gov.uk/education/diversity/ema/

This site has information about the work of Manchester EMAS and ways of supporting EAL pupils in mainstream classrooms. It includes full details of the NASSEA EAL assessment system in its section Supporting New Arrivals

Portsmouth Ethnic Minority Achievement Service
www.blss.portsmouth.sch.uk

This site has been developed by the Portsmouth Ethnic Minority Achievement Service as "a resource base for teachers, parents, educational agencies, students – indeed, anyone with an interest in bilingual education and ethnic minority achievement issues".

Hounslow Language Service
www.ealinhounslow.org.uk

Hounslow EMA Language Service site with downloadable beginners' programmes, multilingual stories, multilingual parents' guides to bilingualism, multilingual maths, key vocabularies, policies and information. Further resources can be purchased from the site.

DfES Ethnic Minority Achievement
www.standards.dfes.gov.uk/ethnicminorities/

The DfES Ethnic Minority Achievement site includes up-to-date information and guidance on raising achievement, ethnic background data collection, useful links information and research on minority ethnic pupils' educational achievements.

EMA Online
www.emaonline.org.uk

This EMA Portal has been developed by Birmingham, Leeds and Manchester LEAs with the help of the DfES to provide resources and support to enable every pupil to fulfil his or her potential. The teaching and learning resources focus on children and young people with English as an additional language and those from minority ethnic backgrounds.

In the Classroom: A toolkit for effective instruction of English learners
www.ncela.gwu.edu/practice/itc/

This toolkit is designed to bring research and practice together for those involved in the education of culturally and linguistically diverse learners. Initiated by the National Clearinghouse for English Language Acquisition in the USA, the project specifically aims to make research-based lessons, activities, and curriculum accessible to all teachers of English language learners (ELLs), whether within bilingual education, ESL, or English-only settings.

The Collaborative Learning Project
www.collaborativelearning.org

This is a network of teaching professionals supporting inclusive education and developing

and disseminating accessible teaching materials in all subject areas and for all ages.

Enchanted Learning
www.enchantedlearning.com

A huge array of free resources to download, which can be used to support bilingual learners in the classroom. Includes bilingual picture dictionaries.

refed – refugee education
www.refed.org.uk

Free discussion forum for teachers and other professionals working with refugee children.

NALDIC – National Association for Language Development in the Curriculum
www.naldic.org.uk

NALDIC provides a professional forum for the teaching and learning of English as an additional language.

2

Developing play opportunities

2 Developing play opportunities

"The After-School Club is just a really good place to have fun. When you just go home it doesn't feel as good. I feel excited when it's time to go to the club. It's nice to get the chance to be creative – it makes you happy. You don't always get that kind of happiness when you're just leaving school to go home at 3.30."

Nivedha, 8, from Sri Lanka

Setting the context

All children have a fundamental right to leisure, play and recreation.

(Article 31, The Convention on the Rights of the Child)

On arrival in the UK, refugee families are often housed in poor-quality, temporary accommodation that is often unsuitable and overcrowded. Some families may have to share a room in a hotel. Poor housing can strain family relationships. Children may also have little or no space to play and are unable to invite friends home.

Many refugee children, like other children from homeless families, miss out on opportunities for play, recreation and making friends – all things that are essential for children's development. Poverty and living on a low income will also restrict access to leisure and recreation opportunities.

High-quality play and recreation opportunities for refugee children are also an important part of any work that aims to help them manage experiences of loss and change. By releasing tension and simply having fun and enjoyment children can often cope better and show resilience. Children can also make friends and develop their language and social skills. Play and creative activities that help refugee children will also, of course, benefit other children, particularly those who are vulnerable.

"When we make nice things it makes me feel good. The grown-ups show us different activities to do, and if I don't do it right, they don't mind. They let me try again until I get it right. When I don't come to after-school club I don't get too sad, but I do get grumpy."

Ahmed, 6, from Somalia

Salusbury WORLD After-School Club

At Salusbury WORLD there is a strong commitment to promoting children's right to leisure, play and recreation. The After-School Club was set up to provide children with play opportunities, creative activities and outlets for self-expression. There have been many positive outcomes for children who attend, including improved confidence and self-esteem, rapid acquisition of English, social skills and academic achievement.

The After-School Club is free for children from refugee families. It is open from 3.30–5.00pm three days a week during term time. Activities include:
- arts and crafts
- sports and games
- music and drama
- trips and outings
- workshops run by outside visitors
- photography
- ICT classes and computer games
- festival and faith projects and celebrations.

Salusbury WORLD After-School Club is run by a play leader with the support of a pool of 15 volunteers.

A successful bid for funding to the Barnardo's Better Play Programme has enabled the After-School Club to run a full-time school holiday programme.

The basics

Many schools will already provide out-of-school-hours learning activities (also known as study support) for their pupils. Out-of-school-hours learning encompasses a wide range of activities outside normal lessons which children take part in voluntarily. It can include such activities as:
- sports, games and outdoor activities
- play
- creative ventures
- homework clubs
- help with key skills, including literacy, numeracy and ICT
- study clubs (linked to or extending curriculum subjects)
- residential events – study weeks or weekends.

Schools may have considerable experience and expertise in developing and sustaining out-of-school-hours provision that may already include refugee children. This existing good practice can be further developed in ways that will improve access and inclusion.

For example, schools could start by evaluating whether membership and attendance at current after-school provision is fully representative of the diversity of the school population

Schools are likely to be familiar already with key national advice, guidance and standards for out-of-school-hours learning (see page 82). This guidance covers areas such as:
- doing an audit
- a whole-school approach
- involving pupils
- involving parents
- health and safety
- funding and resources
- insurance
- child protection
- children with special educational needs
- premises
- internet usage
- adult and pupil ratios
- recruitment and staffing issues
- volunteers
- first aid
- accidents and emergencies.

The following advice may help schools to set up out-of-school-hours activities or expand and develop existing ones.

MEMBERSHIP

Before setting up activities it is important to consider membership criteria, including age range. Schools will also wish to promote

integration by ensuring there is a mix of refugee and non-refugee children.

Staff and volunteers should be aware of the diversity of the school population. Refugee children will come from many different linguistic and cultural backgrounds and will cope with their experiences in different ways. Some children may be new to schooling and may need extra encouragement to get involved in activities.

CHILDREN'S PARTICIPATION

Planning out-of-school-hours learning activities provides a good opportunity to consult children and involve them in decision-making and running groups. Listening to children will help ensure the activities are interesting and engaging. Children can provide feedback and contribute their own ideas for future activities and projects. See **Promoting children's participation** on page 80.

When developing and improving provision, it is essential to have an understanding of the children in the group and to consider their likes, dislikes and ideas. Children should be actively involved in ongoing monitoring, evaluation and review. Staff can elicit feedback from children and parents about activities through listening, discussion and more structured activities. See Children's feedback questionnaire on page 64.

INVOLVING PARENTS

A good working relationship with all parents is vital for the running of any out-of-school-hours activities and clubs. This involves developing trust, respect and understanding. Parents should be kept informed about the type of activities their children are participating in, their value and the progress their children are making. Sharing information and building good communication can make it easier to respond to later concerns.

Good communication with refugee parents is essential. They may be able to help staff to understand the backgrounds and needs of their children, or volunteer help and support. Refugee parents can bring bilingual skills to the group, communicating with children who may be beginners in English. They may also bring an in-depth knowledge of refugee issues, religious beliefs and practices, community activities and organisations. This can increase children's sense of belonging as well as promoting awareness of different languages and cultures.

Refugee parents may be unused to after-school provision and may need persuading of its value.

FUNDING

Schools may be able to draw on a range of sources for funding for any out-of-school-hours provision. In addition to school funds, various sources of additional funding are available. These include the New Opportunities Fund, Friends of the School or PTA, the local education authority, Business in the Community (BITC), Education Business Partnerships, local companies, and trusts and charities. For further information, see **Funding** on page 84.

> As an independent charity, Salusbury WORLD has to apply for funding for its various activities and projects. With no fixed, guaranteed source of funding, project workers need to apply for grants regularly.

HEALTH AND SAFETY

It is essential that activities operate without risk to the health and safety of children, adult helpers and visitors. Health and safety issues, including child protection, should be a key concern in both the planning stage and the ongoing monitoring and review process. All schools should have health and safety policies in place. The issue will also be an integral part of any induction training for adult workers and volunteers. Further advice on this is available in the *Code of Practice for the Primary Sector* (see **National standards and guidance on study support** on page 81) and from the Health and Safety Executive website: www.hse.gov.uk

CHILD PROTECTION

Children and young people have the right to grow up in a safe and caring environment. They have the right to expect adults in positions of responsibility to do everything possible to foster these rights. Child protection issues should be considered in the planning and running of out-of-school activities.

A child protection policy should identify a named person in the setting who will take responsibility for child protection issues. It should set out the appropriate responses from all staff to cases of suspected or alleged abuse and to serious concerns about a child's welfare. More detailed advice on developing a child protection policy is provided in *Safe Keeping: A good practice guide for health and safety in study support* (see **National standards and guidance on study support** on page 81).

Comprehensive guidance from the Department of Health, the Home Office and the Department for Education and Skills is provided in *What to do if you're worried a child is being abused – Children's services guidance* (2003): www.doh.gov.uk/safeguardingchildren/index.htm

STAFFING

The ratio of adults to children will be a key consideration for schools. A care ratio of 1:8 is expected for under-8s. In most local education authorities (LEAs), a recommendation of 1:10 is made for older children.

Staffing is likely to be a mixture of trained play specialists, teachers and volunteers. Recruiting

competent and enthusiastic people will be an important priority. All staff should receive induction on health and safety, child protection and emergency procedures. For further information on recruiting volunteers and developing their work, see **Volunteers** on page 83.

Volunteers are a key resource at Salusbury WORLD After-School Club. In an average week there may be up to ten volunteers supporting paid staff. With an average of 25 children per session, the club would not be able to function without volunteers.

Volunteers are recruited through the school itself, by advertising and by making links with other local community and voluntary sector organisations.

Checks against List 99 (the DfES list of persons banned from working with children) and, where appropriate, criminal records checks should be made on all adults who regularly have contact with children in the course of out-of-school-hours activities. For more information see *Safe Keeping: A good practice guide for health and safety in study support* (see **National standards and guidance on study support** on page 81). The Criminal Records Bureau (CRB) provides a single point of reference for checking criminal records and List 99. Ring the CRB Information Line on 0870 90 90 822 or visit the CRB website: www.crb.gov.uk

PREMISES

Whether the setting intended for use is in a school or elsewhere, it must be suitable for the age group of the children and the activities planned. Initial risk assessments can provide information on any health and safety issues. Children and adults must be provided with a safe, clean and healthy environment. Where possible, the premises available for activities should provide the potential for a range of activities. Good facilities should include indoor creative workspaces, indoor and outdoor space for physical activities, and access to other amenities.

Safe Keeping: A good practice guide for health and safety in study support (see **National standards and guidance on study support** on page 81) provides advice and a pro forma for a premises risk assessment.

RESOURCES, EQUIPMENT AND MATERIALS

To run successful activities staff will need access to a wide range of resources, including art and craft materials, toys, books and sports equipment. When working with refugee children play leaders will find it beneficial to have access to culturally

relevant materials such as artefacts, dual language books and multilingual dictionaries. Particular attention should also be given to any additional requirements of pupils with special educational needs, to ensure they can access and use resources safely. Play leaders must ensure that if children have access to the Internet they will be protected from unsuitable content and inappropriate online contacts.

See **Equipment** on page 88 for information on suppliers.

MONITORING AND EVALUATION

Monitoring and evaluation of provision is essential as it helps to assess whether activities are meeting children's needs. It can also identify the strengths and weaknesses of activities, the views of children, parents and staff, and how improvements can be made.

Monitoring children's attendance and participation can give a clear picture of whether all groups of children are involved fully in activities. It can assist the compilation of summary information that may be needed to present to the school, parents and funders. Crucially, it will also help measure whether projects are having a positive impact on children's lives.

The monitoring and evaluation process does not need to be a complex undertaking, but it does need to be planned. Basic requirements are to record activities, monitor children's well-being and record feedback. Registers, daily logs, weekly programme records, and incident/accident sheets should all be maintained. See **Individual child**

monitoring record, **Daily log**, and **Weekly activity record** on pages 65–67. The *Code of Practice for the Primary Sector* (see **National standards and guidance on study support** on page 81) provides further advice and examples of effective monitoring.

TRAINING AND STAFF DEVELOPMENT

Effective training for staff and volunteer helpers will improve activities and provision. Staff and volunteers may come from a wide range of backgrounds and have different levels of experience and confidence. They will need to be aware of particular issues that may have an impact on refugee children. For example, coping with family separation, changes of accommodation and school, prejudice and language barriers can be stressful for many refugee children, and may, at times, affect their moods and behaviour.

Training may be available locally from LEAs and from other providers, including:

- **The Refugee Council:**
  www.refugeecouncil.org.uk
- **Salusbury WORLD:**
  www.salusburyworld.org.uk
- **Refugee Education Training and Consultancy:**
  www.refugeeeducation.co.uk
- **SkillsActive Playwork Unit:** Information and support for play work and play workers, www.playwork.org.uk.

Activities

The types of activities planned will depend on the needs and experiences of the children who attend. The overall aim should be to provide a wide variety of play, leisure and learning opportunities.

To ensure that activities address the full range of child development needs, play leaders may wish refer to the SPLICE approach (Social, Physical, Language, Intellectual, Creative and Emotional). The SPLICE categories provide a framework for evaluating and auditing provision, and provide pointers for future planning (see **SPLICE activity categories** on page 68 for further information).

Examples of some of the activities that have proved popular and successful in the Salusbury WORLD After-School Club can be found in the activities on pages 69–78.

CREATIVE AND SOCIAL ACTIVITIES, SPORTS AND GAMES

At the Salusbury WORLD After-School Club, activities that foster creativity and freedom of expression help boost children's confidence and self-esteem, and develop their social skills and

"The best thing is getting to do different things all the time."
Dunia, 6, from Iraq

"I like coming to the after-school club because we learn so many skills that we could use maybe when we're older. I feel excited to be able to do new things."
Aurita, 8, from Kosova

capacity for learning. Some refugee children find it easier to communicate feelings and ideas through art, others release negative energy and tension through physical games.

TRIPS AND OUTINGS

Trips and outings are always popular activities that children look forward to. Children can be involved in deciding where to go and planning the trip. Through the year, they can record their ideas for outings on a wall poster (see **Trips and outings suggestions wallchart** on page 79 for a sample chart). Staff and volunteers may not be able to organise exactly what children want, but can usually find something that everyone can enjoy.

Trips and outings are also ideal opportunities to involve refugee parents. They can be involved in planning and can help with supervision and communication. Most important, however, is the chance for a really enjoyable day out.

When planning outings for groups that include refugee children, staff should be aware that some venues and attractions may be unsuitable. For example, children who have lived through a war or violent conflict may not feel comfortable visiting a venue such as the Imperial War Museum. Similarly, a visit to a venue like the London Dungeon may be inappropriate for children whose family members have been victims of human rights abuses, including torture and imprisonment.

SPECIAL EVENTS

Special events can be anything from celebrations of festivals to musical or drama performances. The aim is to ensure that children have variety and challenges.

Special events held to coincide with festivals celebrated by local refugee communities can raise awareness and knowledge of other cultures, and can also help to make connections with the

local community. For example, celebrations of Islamic festivals can provide opportunities to contact Muslim organisations for advice or involvement. Parents may be able to help make these contacts.

JOINT INITIATIVES

A joint initiative is a partnership with one or more outside organisations who can offer the after-school club access to a unique opportunity, activity or facility. The school itself may have something it can offer in return.

The first step is to be aware of organisations and projects in the community that focus on play, leisure or child development, and that could provide interesting activities and opportunities. A friendly approach by phone or in person can help identify what is available, whether there is a shared ethos and whether partnerships are possible.

Both parties will then need to negotiate the practicalities of working together. Key questions to address will include:
- how activities will be paid for
- how the journey will be organised
- how many children can be included
- whether food will be needed
- the specific responsibilities that will be taken by specific staff from each organisation
- the situation regarding insurance.

"The activities are fun and you get lots of help. People come to visit sometimes to do special projects and workshops. There is always something new. It makes me feel happy – like I could do this forever."

Bleron, 8, from Kosova

Salusbury WORLD partnership with St John's Wood Adventure Playground

Although Salusbury WORLD was already providing an extensive range of activities each week, outdoor activities were limited to the space available at school. During the summer, children needed a play space with more features. During autumn and winter, there was also a need for floodlit areas.

A staff member from Salusbury WORLD visited an adventure playground in St John's Wood with indoor and outdoor spaces. Features included pool tables, table tennis tables, a video room, a basketball court, a football space, a digging area, swings and slides, and floodlights.

During a half term, Salusbury WORLD made a three-day trial trip to St John's Wood Adventure

Playground with a small group of children. The days proved to be so popular that both parties developed further plans and a funding application for a joint summer project was developed.

The funding application was successful, with almost £7,000 being granted by the Home Office. Working together, Salusbury WORLD and St John's Wood Adventure Playground used the money to pay for staffing, travel and a summer project promoting refugee integration. Monitoring and evaluation data was also used to develop an application to Barnardo's Better Play Programme for funding for a two-year holiday project. This application was also successful.

Photocopiable resources and activities

Your shout!

Name: _____ Age: _____ Date: _____

Please tell us what you think of your club. Don't be shy!

	YES	NO	DON'T KNOW
Do you enjoy coming to the club?	☐	☐	☐

What things do you like?

_____

_____

What things don't you like?

_____

_____

	YES	NO	DON'T KNOW
Did you feel welcome when you come to the club?	☐	☐	☐
Do you know the names of the staff?	☐	☐	☐
Do you know the club rules?	☐	☐	☐
Do you think the rules are right?	☐	☐	☐
Do you think the activities are good?	☐	☐	☐

What NEW activities would you like to see?

_____

_____

Do you have any ideas for how to improve your club?

_____

_____

Thanks a lot. You are really helpful!

Individual child monitoring record

Name: _____ Age: _____ Date: _____

Country of origin: _____

Attendance (circle as appropriate):   Regular   Occasional

Child's progress
(Play leader comments)

Child's feedback
(Please refer to any comments made on feedback questionnaire)

Does the child enjoy the club?   Yes   No

What does he/she like/dislike about it?

Does he/she have any ideas to improve the club?

Daily log

Date: _____

Play leader(s): _____

Staff/volunteers present: _____

Number of children present: _____

Activities

Other information/incidents

Have you kept examples of children's work? _____

Signed: _____

Weekly activity record

Day	Date	Activities	Groupings	No. of staff required	Preparation	Duration
Monday						
Tuesday						
Wednesday						
Thursday						
Friday						

SPLICE activity categories

SOCIAL

Activities promoting the development of children's social skills. Can include: team building, group/pair exercises, parent participation (eg, family workshops/trips), games and projects that require co-operation.

PHYSICAL

Activities promoting fitness, an awareness of health and the importance of exercise, and the enjoyment of sports. Can include: outside or gym-based running games, sports, team games, performance art, park visits, walks and trips.

LANGUAGE

Activities promoting the development of children's language skills, including using their mother tongue and acquisition of English. Can include: writing/spoken word exercises such as hangman, calligraphy and scrabble, or story time with dual language books.

INTELLECTUAL

Activities promoting the intellectual development of children without being overtly academic. Can include: quizzes, rhyme/proverb writing, flag making, reading, show & tell, festival celebrations and memory games.

CREATIVE

Activities that develop children's creative spirit, promoting freedom to express themselves through a variety of activities. Can include: painting, modelling, photography, animation, music, storytelling, craft, design, performing arts.

EMOTIONAL

Activities that develop self-esteem, confidence, trust and emotional literacy. Can include: trust-building exercises like *Falling* (where one catches a child from behind as they willingly fall) or *Snowstorm* (where a seeing child must guide their blindfolded partner through an obstacle course with words), or communication exercises (Circle Time).

Activity **Back to base**

Description

Back-to-Base is a team game that can be played in any large, clear space such as a hall or playground. It can develop listening skills and familiarity with numbers for children acquiring English as an additional language.

What you need

- a large space
- 8–24 children
- marked out baselines – use chalk, rope, tape or gym benches
- beanbag

How to play

1. Mark out two baselines, one at either end of the space.

2. Line up two teams. For example, with 20 children there will be 10 in each team, Team A and Team B. Give each child a number, ensuring that the matching numbers are of similar age and/or ability. Number 1 on Team A stays at one end of the space, Number 1 on Team B stands at the opposite end. You will then have two groups of 10 facing each other. Call out the numbers 1 – 10 to ensure that each child remembers their number.

3. Place the beanbag in the centre of the space. With each child stationed at their respective baseline, when a number is called, say '4', the two number fours race to get to the beanbag first. The child who grabs the beanbag and returns *Back to Base* earns their team a point. However, the child who fails to reach the beanbag can still win a point by tagging the other child before s/he makes it back to base. *A child can only be tagged if holding the beanbag.* Try playing first team to ten points.

4. Variations:
   (i) Place a hoop or draw a chalk circle around the beanbag and make it a boundary that the competitors cannot overstep. They may reach in only to grab the beanbag. This variation can create hilarious 'wild west'-type stand-offs.
   (ii) Call more than one number at a time. Explain that, once grabbed, the beanbag can be passed or thrown to partners. Likewise, it can be intercepted by opposite numbers. No pushing or shoving is allowed.

Activity **Tunnels**

Description

Tunnels is a variation of tag. It focuses on
co-operation and being aware of the needs of others.

What you need

*   10–20 children
*   a large, clear space, indoor or outdoor, with
    one free wall

How to play

1. Ask for a volunteer to be 'It' or 'On It', and two more to be 'Guards', who
    are interchangeable as 'Catchers'. The rest of the children run from the
    Catchers.

2. If tagged, the child must stand side-on to the wall with their right arm
    outstretched and hand touching the wall. The next child tagged must
    position themselves behind the first, but with their left hand on the first
    child's left shoulder.

3. As a number of children are tagged, they will form a 'tunnel' underneath
    their right arms, between themselves and the wall. The only way to escape is
    for a free runner to tunnel their way under the arms.

4. The guards, starting as catchers, station themselves at either end of the
    human tunnel, in an attempt to stop anyone getting free. If the runners find
    it too difficult, turn a guard into a runner. If the guards find it too difficult,
    do the opposite. Alternatively, use a staff member as a guard or runner. This
    can also help to stop any disputes (who's free, who's not, etc).

5. End the game either if the catchers get everyone, or if the children get tired.

Activity **Cityscape**

Description

Children collaborate to make a model city to hang up in the classroom. Roads, parks, and the skies overhead can be added on later. The activity can help give children a sense of shared neighbourhood, whether it is their own local area, or one in their imagination.

What you need

- a quantity of small cardboard boxes
- cardboard rolls of various sizes
- sheets of card
- brown parcel tape
- tin foil
- glue
- coloured paper
- doll's house paper patterned with bricks, stone and slate
- sticky labels
- string
- scissors
- felt-tip pens

How to make

1. Prepare the boxes by taping up the ends to make them rigid.

2. Pre-cut patterned doll's house paper sheets into convenient sizes. Children can measure the amount of brick paper needed to wrap around the house, and slate paper for around the roof.

3. Glue paper prior to attaching, and use parcel tape to secure the roofs. Use sticky labels for windows, and coloured paper as doors. Kitchen rolls can become aeroplanes, with shapes of cut-out card attached for wings, tails and nose cones. Parcel tape will hold the parts in place.

Activity **Dragon puppets**

Description

Chinese New Year is a spectacularly visual celebration and dragons are an integral part of the proceedings. Children can learn about Chinese cultural traditions at the same time as constructing an animated toy to take home.

What you need

- stiff, lightweight card
- brown parcel tape
- stickers
- glue sticks
- wooden barbecue sticks with the sharp end blunted
- tissue paper
- crayons and felt-tip pens
- scissors
- bradawl

How to make

1. Pre-cut dragons from the card. Each body can be made up of head and upper torso, lower torso and half a tail, two front legs, two back legs, and another length of tail.

2. Using a bradawl, an adult should pierce holes in the four relevant points of connection. Each child will need a set of these body parts, four paper fasteners, and two barbecue sticks.

3. Colour and decorate the body parts before the dragon is assembled.

4. The barbecue sticks can be attached with brown parcel tape to the backs of the two parts of the dragon's torso, which enables it to move.

Further resources

Activity Village – Chinese New Year: www.actvityvillage.co.uk/chinese_new_year.htm

Lots more ideas for games and activities on Chinese New Year.

Portsmouth EMAS: www.blss.portsmouth.sch.uk/hsc/cny/cny.shtml

Wide selection of free downloadable resources.

Activity **Graphic collages**

Description

This activity enables children to explore graphic design and collage techniques. They can also explore different scripts. Calligraphy and the decorative use of words are important in many cultures.

What you need

- a selection of different types of paper: silver, gold, metallic, embossed
- newspaper headlines, if possible in different languages with different scripts
- glue sticks
- pens
- alphabet stencils
- graphic stickers – eg, stars

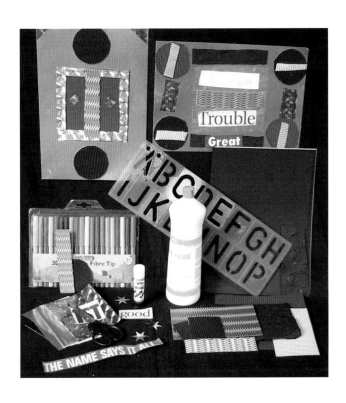

How to make

1. Each child needs an A4 sheet of lightweight card or paper in a striking colour.

2. Pre-cut all other paper materials into manageable sizes.

3. Talk about symmetry, and how a short headline can change the visual message.

Activity **Masks**

Description

Mask-making combines art and drama, and makes it possible for the children to transform themselves in moments. The rich traditions of mask-making in cultures from around the world can also be explored, highlighting common cultural themes.

What you need

- paper plates
- glue sticks
- brown parcel tape
- felt-tip pens
- crayons
- chalks
- scissors
- feathers
- rug wool
- strips of paper, ribbon or thin elastic
- barbecue sticks with the sharp end blunted

How to make

1. Cut paper plates into mask shapes – birds, lions, tigers, cats, monkeys and bears. Younger children may need to use pre-cut paper plates. Cut out eyeholes and pre-staple on ears and beaks.

2. Decorate with colours and glue on materials.

3. Attach a barbecue stick onto the back of the mask with brown parcel tape. (Stick masks are easier to fit to an individual's face so that they can see out.)

Further resources

Making Masks
ISBN: 1550749315
Published by Kids Can Press

Africa: Eyewitness guide
by Yvonne Ayo
£9.99, ISBN 0751360554
Published by Dorling Kindersley
Available from: www.dk.com

Activity **The sea**

Description

A group project that creates a colourful display and reflects the satisfaction to be gained from working together. Children can use books and the Internet to research sea creatures and marine life.

What you need

- cardboard rolls of varying sizes – eg, loo rolls, kitchen rolls
- blue and clear bubble wrap
- template of octopus and starfish
- textured silver paper
- silver glitter
- silver paint
- sticky dots
- tissue paper
- brushes
- scissors
- glue sticks
- real shells
- toy crabs, jellyfish, etc.

How to make

1. Pre-cut the cardboard rolls, making an indentation for the fish mouth at one end. Staple the other end over a fishtail shape, cut from flat card.

2. Provide textured silver wrapping paper for fins, and sticky dots or crumpled tissue paper for eyes.

3. Paint the assembled fish with silver paint, and glue on a bit of glitter for iridescence.

4. Pin together closely in the shape of a shoal with long pins, and attach to a display board. The board can be lined with blue wrapping paper, blue bubble wrap, clear bubble wrap and a few bits of cotton wool to give the impression of waves at the top of the sea.

5. Children may then choose to make another creature, such as a starfish, with crumpled tissue paper glued on for texture, or an octopus, a dolphin, a shell or crab.

Further resources

DK Guide to the Ocean
by Francis Dipper
£9.99, ISBN 0751344494
Published by Dorling Kindersley
Available from: www.dk.com

Activity **Sock puppets**

Description

Puppet shows are an almost universal form of entertainment for children. The making of puppets can draw on a wide diversity of materials, from paper and sticks to socks, gloves or fabric. Children love to construct a character that can come to life at will. Play with puppets can also foster language use, with the puppet doing the talking, and can help children to express difficult emotions.

What you need

- old socks
- felt sheets
- paper cups
- scissors
- glue sticks
- decorative bits and pieces – eg, fuzzy pom-poms or packages of wobbly eyes

How to make

1. Pre-cut out sheets of felt into smaller squares. If working with very young children pre-cut ears, eyes, tongues, noses and spots.

2. Insert a paper cup in the toe of the sock and glue on features with glue sticks.

Further resources

The world of puppets
www.itdc.sbcss.k12.ca.us/curriculum/
puppetry.html

A website with lesson plans and ideas for exploring puppets from around the world.

Puppets by Post
www.puppetsbypost.com

A huge range of puppets available by post.

Parrotfish
www.parrotfish.co.uk

Multicultural puppet resources.

Positive Identity
www.positive-identity.com

Multicultural toys and puppets, including black and Asian finger puppets.

Activity **Still life collage**

Description

This activity can be used to introduce the children to fruits from many different parts of the world. Children can taste the fruits after the activity.

What you need

- a selection of visually interesting fruit – eg, watermelon, orange, lemon, kiwi fruit, papaya, grapes
- a serving platter
- cutlery, serviettes and platters cut from brightly coloured paper
- glue sticks
- coloured chalk
- black tissue crumpled into tiny balls for seeds

How to make

1. Prepare a platter of cut fruit, using those with strong colours, patterns and striking seed formations.

2. The children can either cut out the fruit shapes themselves, or use pre-cut ones if time is limited.

3. Use the chalk to add shading on the rinds and peels.

4. Glue on real watermelon seeds or bits of crumpled black tissue paper.

Activity **Mosaics**

Description

Mosaics can be made from small ceramic tiles to look more traditional. A simple motif, such as the first letter of the child's name, produces the best results. Show children pictures of mosaics through history, from Roman and Byzantine times, to illustrate how widespread the craft of mosaic-making is across the world.

What you need

- thin chipboard sheets (a builder's merchant will cut into suitable sized rectangles)
- sheets of mosaic tiles in various colours
- PVA adhesive
- ceramic wall tile grout
- optional small glass pebbles or bits of mirror
- hand tile snippers

How to make

1. Separate the tiles from the sheets. Some can be pre-cut into halves or quarters by an adult, using the tile snippers. (Take care, the edges may be sharp.)

2. Draw the desired design onto the board.

3. Apply glue to the back of each tile and stick down onto the board. Encourage the children to cover the whole surface with tiles and to line the outer edges of the rectangle with a frame of tiles.

4. When the adhesive is completely dry, grout the entire surface, and carefully wipe clean with a damp cloth.

Further resources

Classic Mosaic: Inspiration from 4,000 BC to 2,000 AD
by Elaine Goodwin
£12.99, ISBN 1840923288
Published by Apple Press

The Mosaic Decorator's Sourcebook: Over 100 designs to copy and create
by Rosalind Wates
£15.99, ISBN 0715311395
Published by David and Charles

Trips and outings suggestions wallchart

Where do YOU want to go?	Name

Further information and resources

Promoting children's participation

Working together: Giving children and young people a say (2004)
www.publications.teachernet.gov.uk

This guidance from the DfES provides a basis for involving children and young people in decisions affecting all aspects of the life of the school. It includes examples of good practice for schools to use and adapt as they choose.

Participation – Spice it Up!: Practical tools for engaging children and young people in planning and consultations (2002)
£18.95, ISBN 1 84187 062 5
Published by Save the Children

Packed full of practical tools and ideas for engaging children and young people.

Children are Service Users Too: A guide for consulting children and young people (2004)
£4.95, ISBN 1 84187 086 2
Published by Save the Children

A practical guide aimed at organisations looking for ways to consult children and young people. It is particularly aimed at organisations applying for the Charter Mark who need to involve children and young people in their consultation of service users.

Children as Partners in Planning: A training resource to support consultation with children (2000)
£15, ISBN 1 84187 031 5
Published by Save the Children

This practical training manual is aimed at childcare workers in a range of settings.

A Journey of Discovery (1999)
£6.50, ISBN 1 84187 013 7
Published by Save the Children

This pack describes a consultation project in London's East End. It outlines: the thinking that needs to be done before starting a consultation; setting up a partnership approach; how the project was introduced to the children; consultation ideas; evaluation activities; and activity sheets and materials.

National standards and guidance on Study Support (out-of-school-hours learning)

DfES Study Support Homepage
www.standards.dfes.gov.uk/studysupport

The Study Support Website offers schools, teachers and LEAs support and advice about initiating and continuing good practice in out-of-school-hours learning throughout primary and secondary education.

DfES Study Support Toolkit – Making it work in schools (2000)
www.standards.dfes.gov.uk/studysupport/docs/toolkitschls

The *Study Support Toolkit* is a package of materials that provides practical self-development and training resources to help headteachers and study support co-ordinators in schools and local authorities develop or expand their study support programmes.

Study Support Code of Practice (2004)
www.standards.dfes.gov.uk/studysupport/news/?newsID=929945

The new code of practice brings together for the first time, guidance for primary, secondary and special schools. Many schools have extended and improved their study support provision and the involvement of pupils, parents and other partners. The changes incorporated in this new and revised reflect these developments.

Safe Keeping – A good practice guide for health and safety in study support (2000)
www.standards.dfes.gov.uk/studysupport/docs/safekeep

This guide gives practical advice and information on tackling a wide range of issues, from food hygiene to volunteer recruitment, and will be useful for new and existing programmes.

Guidance on First Aid in Schools (1998)
www.teachernet.gov.uk/management/healthandsafety/firstaid/

A good practice guide that provides advice for schools on drawing up first aid policies and ensuring they are meeting their statutory duties. It includes a checklist of issues which schools may find helpful when undertaking a risk assessment.

The Essential Guide to Summer Schools (2000)
www.standards.dfes.gov.uk/studysupport/docs/esssum

A guide based on the experiences of 25 summer school pilot projects funded by the DfES. The guide covers planning, setting up and running summer schools.

Setting up out-of-school-hours learning

ContinYou
www.continyou.org.uk

ContinYou (formerly Education Extra) publishes a series of 'How To' pamphlets which provide an A–Z of setting up and running popular and successful clubs in your school. Titles currently available are:
How to Run a Successful Reading Club
How to Run a Successful Environment Club
How to Run a Successful History Club
How to Run a Successful Visual Arts Club
How to Run a Successful Science Club.

Each pack describes in detail the steps to take to set up and sustain the club plus a pamphlet on funding, health and safety, monitoring and added learning. A lively and witty poster of specific club activities accompanies each pack, plus up-to-date lists of websites and partner organisations in each subject.

Price: £5 each, or three packs for the price of two. Contact Lisa Warren at ContinYou on 020 8709 9901.

Kid's Clubs Network
www.kidsclubs.com

Kids' Clubs Network is the national organisation for out-of-school childcare. The organisation offers advice and support to out-of-school clubs, parents, children, childcare providers, national government, local authorities, employers and Early Years Development and Childcare Partnerships.

Quality in Study Support
www.qiss.org.uk

Quality in Study Support (QiSS) helps schools, LEAs, community groups and other organisations to raise students' achievement, motivation and self-esteem by improving the quality of out-of-school-hours learning. QiSS offers a range of services including consultancy, training, research, publications, events and a quality assurance scheme for study support providers.

Breakfast Clubs
www.breakfast-club.co.uk

The Breakfast Club website provides information needed to set up and run a successful breakfast club. On the 'resources' part of the site you can download *Breakfast Clubs: A how to guide*, which gives advice on how to plan your club; information on diet and nutrition; advice on how to find funding; and tips on how to make use of other resources.

Volunteers

National Centre for Volunteering
www.volunteering.org.uk

Offers comprehensive information about all aspects of volunteering and links to organisations that provide volunteering opportunities.

The National Centre for Volunteering publishes *The A–Z of Volunteering and Asylum*. This is a practical handbook for people managing volunteers who work with refugees or asylum-seekers, or managing volunteers who are refugees or asylum-seekers (price £12).

Millennium Volunteers
www.mvonline.gov.uk

This government-backed initiative encourages 16–24-years-olds to get involved in local issues that they care about.

Community Service Volunteers
www.csv.org.uk

CSV is a UK charity dedicated to giving everyone the chance to play an active part in their community through volunteering. The website has information on a wide range of volunteering opportunities.

TimeBank
www.timebank.org.uk

This national volunteering campaign raises awareness of giving time through voluntary work. By registering with TimeBank, your interests and skills will be matched to volunteering opportunities in your local area.

Do-it
www.do-it.org.uk

Do-it.org.uk has a database of local volunteering opportunities sorted by postcode, type of work and type of organisation.

Jobs In Charities
www.jobsincharities.co.uk

Volunteer vacancies are advertised in a section in this charity recruitment advertising site.

Funding

The Children's Fund Local Network
www.cypu.gov.uk

The Children's Fund was set up by the Government to tackle poverty and social exclusion. The Local Network provides grants for local and community groups tackling poverty and disadvantage among children and young people.

The Schools Funding Guide (2001)
www.dsc.org.uk/acatalog/Schools.html

This guide lists over 200 potential sources of funding for primary and secondary schools in the maintained and independent sectors. Whether you are looking to raise a modest sum, or planning a major appeal, this book will help you devise and carry out a fundraising strategy that works.

School Financial Management
www.optimus.co.uk

A monthly magazine for schools providing information on all available funding opportunities.

Awards for All
www.awardsforall.org.uk

This is a Lottery grant programme aimed at local communities. They award grants of between £500 and £5,000 to "projects which involve people in their local community, bringing them together to enjoy arts, sports and charity activities", in a simple straightforward way. You can apply through a short and simple application form on the website, and there are links to guidance notes and sources of help.

Barnardo's Better Play
www.barnardos.org.uk/betterplay/

Barnardo's and the Children's Play Council are working in partnership to deliver Better Play – a four-year £10.8 million England-wide grant programme funded by the New Opportunities Fund. Objectives include addressing the play needs of particularly disadvantaged groups.

Kellogg's Breakfast Club Awards
www.breakfast-club.co.uk

The Breakfast Club Awards offer breakfast clubs across the UK the opportunity to apply for funding and receive recognition for their work.

The Awards offer three levels of funding:
- 30 Start Up awards of £500 for new or recently established clubs
- 20 Expansion Awards worth £1,000 for clubs looking to develop their existing provision
- eight Excellence awards of £2,500 for clubs demonstrating best practice.

Camelot Foundation

www.camelotfoundation.org.uk

The focus of the Camelot Foundation's work is young people aged 11–25 who have slipped out of the mainstream of society, or who are in danger of doing so. Young asylum-seekers are a priority group for grants under the 'Transforming Lives' programme.

Comic Relief

www.comicrelief.com

The Comic Relief UK grants programme aims to tackle poverty and promote social justice by helping people make lasting, positive changes in their lives and communities. Priorities in the period from 2003–2005 include projects that support young people and refugees and asylum-seekers.

The Big Lottery Fund

www.biglotteryfund.org.uk

Big Lottery Fund was created by merging the New Opportunities Fund and the Community Fund. It will hand out half the money for good causes from the National Lottery. Through the Young People's Fund, support is available for projects that will improve local communities and offer more opportunities to young people.

Excellence in Cities (EiC)

www.standards.dfes.gov.uk/sie/eic/

EiC operates in England only and is a targeted programme to bring additional resources to core urban areas. If you are in an EiC area, additional funding from the Standards Fund will support study support initiatives. EiC brings a new approach that: increases the diversity of provision for pupils and at the same time encourages schools to co-operate to raise standards; extends learning opportunities for pupils of all abilities; and, above all, starts with the needs of individual pupils and the challenges they face.

Funder Finder

www.funderfinder.org.uk

FunderFinder develops and distributes software to help individuals and not-for-profit organisations in the UK identify charitable trusts that might give them money.

Access Funds UK

www.access-funds.co.uk

This website aims to provide the latest funding information from central government, National Lottery, devolved governing bodies, the EU and quangos. Access Funds has a range of services to help you fundraise. These include email services and training courses. The website also contains directories of funding programmes and guides to funding.

Rotary International

www.ribi.org

Rotary International is the world's largest service organisation for business and professional people. Local districts and clubs may show an interest in supporting projects and initiatives.

Lions Clubs International

www.lions.org.uk

Lions Clubs International is a community service organisation. Lions Clubs prioritise the needs of vulnerable young people through Lions Youth Programmes.

Activities

100 Games & Activities for the School Playground
(1997)
£7.50, ISBN 1 873928 23 8
Published by Learning Design
www.learningdesign.biz

This book details 100 traditional games, from
Cat and Mouse to Silver River. It can be be used
in a wide variety of settings and by those working
in nurseries, play centres, after-school clubs and
adventure playgrounds.

London Play
www.londonplay.org.uk

London Play is a London-wide voluntary
organisation that supports and co-ordinates
out-of-school play services for children across
London.

UK Children's Directory
www.ukchildrensdirectory.com

This is a comprehensive directory of websites for
children's services and activities throughout the

UK. Some sites may be international sites, hosted
in other countries, but nevertheless of interest to
parents, carers, teachers and children in the UK.

Beetroot
www.beetroot.org.uk

Beetroot provides information and resources to
support arts and environmental learning in out-
of-school-hours in London.

Days Out UK
www.days-out.co.uk

The Days Out UK website provides information
on family days out around the UK.

Shap online calendar of religious festivals
www.support4learning.org.uk/shap

Equipment

Acorn Educational
www.acorneducational.co.uk

Supplier of educational toys and games for children under six years of age and children with special needs.

Positive Identity
www.positive-identity.com

Multicultural toys, dolls, books, puppets and posters.

East-West Education
www.eastwesteducation.org

Suppliers of traditional Asian and African clothing for dolls and children.

Articles of Faith
www.articlesoffaith.co.uk

Articles of Faith is the leading supplier of religious artefacts and resources for education by mail order.

The Festival Shop
www.festivalshop.co.uk

The Festival Shop provides multi-faith calendars, books, posters and other resources.

Tamarind
www.tamarindbooks.co.uk

Publisher of multicultural children's books.

NES Arnold
www.nesarnold.co.uk

General resources and equipment supplier.

The Parrotfish Company
www.parrotfish.co.uk

The Parrotfish Company supplies authentic multicultural artefacts and accompanying educational materials, such as photo-packs.

3

Involving refugee parents

3 Involving refugee parents

"Both my wife and I were very impressed with the warm welcome we received from Mrs Carol Munro, the headteacher, and her staff. Instantly, we understood that this is the right school for our children and the best place for them to feel at home, as we came from overseas."

Sabri, parent from Albania

Setting the context

As a result of the Race Relations (Amendment) Act 2000, schools now have specific duties to promote race equality and ensure that they monitor the impact of their policies on different groups of children and parents. Schools should, therefore, check the quality of their links with the parents of refugee children, and whether they are positively encouraged to play a full part in the life and development of the school. Their involvement in a wide range of school activities should be actively monitored.

> "The best schools engage constructively with parents, treating them as equal partners in their children's education. They look imaginatively at ways to encourage dialogue and listen to parents. Above all, they make parents welcome and respond respectfully to their needs and concerns."
>
> Aiming High: Raising the achievement of minority ethnic pupils, Department for Education and Skills, 2003

There are many reasons why refugee parents might be less likely to be involved in their children's education than other groups of parents. Refugee parents may:

- be unable to communicate in English
- be unfamiliar with the education system in Britain and how children are taught
- be unaware of how to support their children's learning
- come from a culture where there is no tradition or expectation of parental involvement
- be feeling stressed because of dislocation and the pressure of applying for asylum
- be experiencing poverty
- not have access to materials and resources at home
- live in poor-quality and overcrowded accommodation
- have frequent changes of home and school when living in temporary or emergency accommodation.

The school environment should be welcoming for refugee families, but establishing trusting relationships with parents often takes time. A warm initial welcome, along with supportive procedures for interview and admission, will help build good communication and partnership between the school and home. If refugee parents feel genuinely welcomed and are given the information and support they need, they generally show tremendous support for schools and encourage and motivate their children.

Involving refugee parents at Salusbury WORLD

Salusbury Primary School welcomes the diversity of its pupils' backgrounds and acknowledges the positive contribution that all children make to the school.

Salusbury WORLD supports the ethos of the school by encouraging the participation of refugee parents. We believe that the involvement of refugee parents in school life is an effective means of ensuring the educational success of pupils and improving their well-being.

At Salusbury WORLD parents have become involved in supporting their children's learning. Some parents have become volunteers and help at the After School Club. Others help with translations and interpretation and with administrative tasks. Parents have also spoken about their experiences at conferences, workshops, and fundraising events.

Parents are encouraged to give feedback on the services provided by Salusbury WORLD and some have become members of our Board of Trustees.

Communicating effectively with parents

Schools should develop a range of strategies to promote good relationships with refugee parents. It may be necessary to try different approaches, as it can take time to find a system of communication that works best for the school and the parent. Schools will benefit from investing time in listening to parents and understanding their concerns.

Good communication with parents is everyone's responsibility and all staff need to be involved in training sessions on parental involvement. The following strategies are helpful in supporting good home–school communication.

- Ensure that the school conducts an annual survey of pupils' first languages. Local communities are becoming more linguistically diverse and schools should be aware of the languages spoken in the local community.
- Build up contacts and resources for interpreting, including volunteers from the school community and local professional interpreting services.
- Organise interpreters for admission interviews, parent conferences and parents' evenings. Letting parents know in advance that an interpreter will be present has been shown to boost attendance. See **Guidelines for using interpreters** on page 26, which has information and guidance on using

"The people at school are helpful and friendly. They've always got time for me."
Deka, parent from Somalia

interpreters in admission interviews and other meetings with parents and carers.

- Provide translations of important letters.
- In letters sent home, use simple and direct language, whether translated or not.
- Use illustrations to make letters more easily understandable.
- Explain the contents of letters to parents and pupils (if appropriate).
- Talk to parents and carers personally when inviting them to school events.
- Remind parents about a school event on the day it is going to take place. Telephone reminders can also help.

Creating opportunities for parents to get involved

A school that already enjoys a high level of parental involvement will be well placed to promote the involvement of newly arrived refugee parents.

It is essential to consult parents about their needs and the kinds of support and activities they want rather than make assumptions about what would benefit families. Consultation will ensure better understanding, genuine participation, and better attendance and support for school events.

Activities that promote parental involvement include the following.

CLASS TRIPS

Parents enjoy the chance to help on trips, as it is a way of getting to know the class and the teacher. They may also appreciate the opportunity to have an enjoyable day out with other children and parents.

ASSEMBLIES, CELEBRATIONS AND FUN EVENTS

Many schools regularly welcome parents to school assemblies. By inviting parents to stay on afterwards the school can disseminate information and provide opportunities for parents to get to know each other. School assemblies can also celebrate festivals and other events. Parents can be invited to help and participate.

SOCIAL EVENTS

One of the most successful and best-attended events in many schools is an 'International Evening'. Attendance is better if parents are involved in the planning. They may also be aware of local cultural resources, such as musicians and dancers.

Parents can be asked to bring food from their country of origin, although schools should be sensitive to families in difficult circumstances, including those living in bed and breakfast accommodation where there may be no access to cooking facilities. Free school events ensure that parents on low incomes are not excluded.

HELPING IN SCHOOL

Parents who are able to help and volunteer in school can help to increase their children's confidence and, if given the right opportunities, can raise the profile of their own community. Refugee parents have many skills that schools will welcome and value. For some parents, helping or volunteering in school can act as a springboard towards employment or further education. For information on volunteering projects and organisations, see **Volunteers** on page 83.

READING TOGETHER

Parents can be welcomed to story-time sessions in schools and invited to tell or read a story in their home language. Schools can also support home reading by lending books and other resources. See page 100 for examples of resources for home reading activities.

BOOK AND STORY TAPE-MAKING

Parents can be invited to take part in book and story tape-making activities with their children. Book-making sessions can be used to record class outings, activities and special events, and to write stories and autobiographies. Completed books can be translated by parents and made available to classes as dual language resources.

FAMILY LEARNING

See page 100 for information on family learning.

Creating supportive networks

Refugee parents can and do provide each other with help and support. Schools are often the hub of community and family networks and can provide isolated parents with many opportunities to connect with others and begin to feel part of a community.

School staff should try to learn about the backgrounds of local refugee communities and be sensitive to differences and possible conflicts. It should not be assumed that because they share a language or nationality, families will necessarily wish to mix and develop closer links. By listening and getting to know parents, schools will develop this knowledge and understanding.

Schools can encourage parental networking by:
- developing the role of a parental involvement co-ordinator to support parent networks and resource their activities
- involving non-refugee parents as volunteers – this can foster a greater awareness of refugees' needs and promote communication and links in the local community
- working with the Parent–Teacher Association (PTA) to build up supportive networks within the school
- holding coffee mornings at regular intervals to extend a PTA welcome to parents who are new to the school
- linking up with other local schools through joint initiatives and sharing successful practice
- providing space within the school for mother-tongue language classes and supplementary schools.

Space permitting, a room could be made available for use by parents. Multilingual resources and information can also be displayed here. A parents' noticeboard can be provided if no room is available.

Family learning

School-based family learning activities can enable parents to become more involved in their children's learning. They can help parents understand how children are taught in school and also improve parents' literacy, numeracy and ICT skills. Family learning activities can also include parenting education, educational visits, and art, music and sporting activities.

> Salusbury WORLD provided space for sewing classes organised by the local adult education department. These were very popular and provided a useful qualification for the parents as well as social opportunities.

Consulting and listening to parents can help identify priorities and inform planning. Family learning activities should be tailored to suit the needs of particular groups of parents or address concerns identified by the school.

Tuition and funding are available for many family learning activities. A teacher or school-based professional should coordinate and liaise with family learning providers to ensure that programmes are linked to school priorities for inclusion and parental involvement. Schools should monitor attendance at family learning activities to ensure that all sections of the community are involved and are benefiting from the activities.

When planning activities, schools need to consider the following points:
- Identify which parents will be invited to attend. Time and effort should be put into the process of communication, publicity and recruitment.
- Set a time to suit the maximum number of parents.
- Keep a register of everyone who attends and record their ethnic background.
- Provide interpreters if needed.
- Crèche facilities should be offered to ensure that parents with young children are not excluded. If this is not possible, younger siblings should be offered toys to play with in the same room.
- Build in time at the end of session for feedback. Be prepared to adapt activities in response.

- Ensure there is enough time at the end of sessions for parents to socialise with each other. This is always enjoyable and may be just as important for parents as the learning activities.

Popular family learning activities include:

FAMILY LITERACY AND NUMERACY WORKSHOPS

The Basic Skills Agency is the leading agency for family programmes funded by the Learning and Skills Council. LEAs are offered funding for a range of programmes including Family Literacy workshops, Family Numeracy workshops and Keeping up with the Children. More information can be found on the Basic Skills Agency's Skills for Families website: www.skillsforfamilies.org

Further examples of family literacy programmes that schools may find useful include:
- Books for Babies
- Storysack projects
- Reading is Fundamental.

See page 100 for more information on these types of projects.

CURRICULUM WORKSHOPS

Curriculum workshops can provide parents with an introduction to the Foundation Stage (nursery and reception classes) and the National Curriculum. Workshops can also cover topics such as homework, national tests (SATs), learning EAL, special needs and ways that parents can help with learning.

Refugee parents who have recently arrived in the UK may be unfamiliar with the content of the school curriculum. They may also be unaware that in the UK children are placed in classes according to age, and not as a result of tests.

Developing activities and resources for refugee and other minority ethnic parents will help provide useful resources for the whole school community.

The DfES series of *Learning Journey* guides for parents provides information about the Foundation Stage and the National Curriculum, and tips for how parents can help children at home. They are available in many languages and also in audio cassette, Braille and large print versions. The Learning Journeys have their own orderline, telephone 0800 096 6626 or visit www.parentcentre.gov.uk/learningjourneys

BEHAVIOUR WORKSHOPS

These can be developed flexibly in response to the needs of parents. Topics can include:
- parents' expectations of how the school promotes good behaviour
- ways of managing behavioural problems
- discussing children's experiences of racism and bullying and how the school responds.

PUPIL LITERACY WORKSHOPS

These can help parents support their children's reading and writing at home. Topics can include:
- using dual language books for home reading and activities
- ways of maintaining home languages
- explaining the school reading scheme

- providing information about local library services, or visiting the library
- explaining how the school teaches reading and uses reading records
- showing parents how they can help their children by talking about books and pictures even if they are not confident in English.

EDUCATIONAL ADVICE SESSIONS

Parents may wish to discuss matters which concern their own child. Some teachers set aside an hour at the end of the school day, once a week, when they make themselves available to talk to parents.

Parents' evenings

Parents may need information about parents' evenings and how to respond to invitation letters. Schools may wish to explore further ways to promote attendance rather than simply sending letters home. Some parents are more likely to attend if they know that an interpreter will be present.

Schools should check whether there are parents who were unable to attend and try to reschedule appointments where possible.

At Salusbury WORLD, the Home–School Liaison Worker helps parents to understand what happens during a parents' evening, ensures appointments are booked and that interpreters are arranged when needed. Parents' attendance is also monitored.

Further information and resources

Guidance on parental involvement

The Standards Site: Parental Involvement
www.standards.dfes.gov.uk/parentalinvolvement

A DfES website which offers suggestions on how to achieve effective partnership with parents and how best to manage and use home–school agreements.

National Confederation of Parent Teacher Organisations
www.ncpta.org.uk

The NCPTA offers advice on setting up and running a Parent Teacher Association and the legal requirements of running events. It also publishes comprehensive fact sheets.

Involving parents, raising achievement
www.teachernet.gov.uk/wholeschool/
familyandcommunity/workingwithparents/
ipratoolkit/

The IPRA booklet contains information and ideas to help you develop successful home-school links. Although it was written with secondary schools in mind, most of the ideas contained in the booklet apply equally well in primary schools and special schools.

Improving Parental Involvement (2003)
by Garry Hornby
£19.99, ISBN: 0826470254
Published by Continuum International Publishing Group

A practical book that provides information and ideas to help teachers increase parental involvement.

School, Family, Community: Mapping school inclusion in the UK (1999)
by Alan Dyson and Elaine Robson
£13.95, ISBN: 086155213X
Published by National Youth Agency

This report reviews the literature on parental involvement in children's learning. It examines communication between home and school, school support for families, and the collaboration between schools and the local community.

Family learning

Basic Skills Agency
www.basic-skills.co.uk

The Basic Skills Agency is the national development organisation for literacy and numeracy in England and Wales

Basic Skills Agency Family Learning Programmes
www.skillsforfamilies.org

An overview of funding and types of programmes.

National Institute of Adult Continuing Education (NIACE)
www.niace.org.uk

NIACE publishes a number of resources to support family learning projects, including:

Learning Legacies: A guide to family learning (2000)
£9.95, ISBN: 1 86201 107 9

This book provides a detailed account of family learning in practice, from the early stage of getting started through to funding provision and quality assurance. There are examples of good practice and case studies drawn from a wide range of family learning settings.

Walking Ten Feet Tall (2001)
£60, ISBN: 1 86201 132 X

A comprehensive set of photocopiable materials designed to support family learning practitioners in a range of settings.

ContinYou
www.continyou.org.uk

The ContinYou website is a source of information on family learning projects and publications.

Campaign for Learning
www.campaign-for-learning.org.uk

The Campaign for Learning works for an inclusive society in which learning is understood, valued and accessible to everyone. Its website provides links to many resources for family learning practitioners.

Centre for Literacy in Primary Education (CLPE)
www.clpe.co.uk/familylearning/familylearning.html

The CLPE is an educational centre for schools and teachers, parents and teaching assistants. The CLPE has established a significant and growing role in working with parents and have developed a range of family learning initiatives and publications.

London Language and Literacy Unit (LLLU)
www.sbu.ac.uk/lllu

The LLLU is a national consultancy and professional development centre for staff working in the areas of literacy, numeracy, dyslexia, family learning and English for Speakers of Other Languages.

The Literacy Trust
www.literacytrust.org.uk

Contains a guide to, and a directory of, materials for family literacy and resources for parents.

Story Sacks

A *Storysack* is a large cloth bag containing a good-quality children's picture book with supporting materials to stimulate reading activities. It also contains soft toys of the main characters and props and scenery relating to the story to bring the book to life. A non-fiction book linked to the fiction theme, an audio tape and a language game based on the book are included. These can be provided in a variety of languages with the help of the local community. Additionally, there are ideas for parents and teachers to develop children's speaking, listening, reading and writing skills using the contents of the *Storysack*.

Storysacks can be made by parents and volunteers or purchased as ready-made resources from: EDS Ltd, Resource House, Kay Street, Bury, Lancashire, Tel: 0161 763 6232

Storysacks: A starter information pack (2001) This pack is a useful resource for groups or individuals who wish to start their own *Storysack* library. The pack includes detailed advice on: how to make *Storysack* sacks including useful craft and design hints; how to attract and organise volunteer help; where to acquire sponsorship and funding; and promotional activities and training workshops for parents. Additionally it offers a pull-out photocopiable guide for parents on how to use *Storysacks* and includes patterns for making soft toy characters and letter stencils for labelling the sacks.

Price: £15 plus post & packing. Available from: Neil Griffiths, Director, National Project for Storysacks, c/o Pinehurst Infant School, Beech Avenue, Swindon, Wiltshire SN2 1JT.

Reading Is Fundamental UK
www.literacytrust.org.uk/rif

Reading Is Fundamental (RIF) UK is an initiative of the National Literacy Trust which helps children and young people to realise their potential by motivating them to read. In RIF projects, children choose three free books a year. They also receive a book box, bookmarks, bookplates and badges. Book distributions are accompanied by fun, high-quality activities, often involving authors, poets, storytellers and illustrators, which emphasise the pleasures of reading.

RIF currently operates two national programmes:
• All Books for Children – a partnership scheme that provides opportunities for families to attend RIF events at their local library. www.literacytrust.org.uk/rif/aboutrif/allbooksforchildren.htm
• Shared Beginnings – an 11-week programme that parents practical ideas for supporting their children's early language and literacy through conversation, play, making books and using local community resources. www.literacytrust.org.uk/rif/aboutrif/sharedbeginnings.htm

Let's Read (1999)
A simple dual language guide that sets out ways in which parents can encourage their children to become confident readers. Guidance includes information on:
- how talking paves the way for reading
- how to foster a love of books
- bilingualism as an asset
- reading is not just about books
- reading in schools
- how to use libraries.

Guides are available in the following languages: Albanian, Arabic, Bengali, Chinese, French, Gujarati, Punjabi, Portuguese, Serbo-Croat, Somali, Spanish, Tamil, Turkish, Urdu.

Price £6.99. Available from www.mantralingua.com

Materials from Learning Design
www.learningdesign.biz
- *Reading Together* (2002)
  A 12-page A5 guide which offers user-friendly advice to parents on helping their children to acquire and consolidate their reading skills. Available in Albanian, Bengali, English, French, Romany and Somali. Price £3.

- *Helping Your Child to Learn at Home and at School: A guide for bilingual parents* (1999) Available in Albanian, Bengali, English and Somali editions
  Price: £3 plus £0.60 post & packing
- *Parents in Primary Schools* (1996)
  These materials aim to convey, in an interactive way, a real understanding of how primary schools work. The materials could be used as induction for parents of children about to start school, parents involved in running toy libraries, after school clubs, parents in ESOL or basic skills classes or in training sessions for parent governors.
  Price £6 plus £1 post & packing.

Help Your Child to Succeed: An essential guide for parents (2002)
by Bill Lucas and Alistair Smith

A guide for parents of pre-school and primary children. Packed with activities, games, tips and suggestions for supporting and helping children succeed in school.

Published by: Network Educational Press, Box 635, Stafford ST16 1BF. Tel: 01785 225515, www.networkpress.co.uk

Advice and information for parents

UK Education Guide
www.ukeducationguide.co.uk

Links to education and homework sites.

BBC Education Dynamo
www.bbc.co.uk/education/dynamo/parents/
index.shtml
A site for parents who want to help their
5–9-year-olds learn at home.

Spark Island
www.sparkisland.com

A guide to interactive, fun educational products
for schools and homes with children aged 3–11,
which consolidate and improve core subject skills.
The range includes online services, CD-ROMs,
books and a magazine. The site has sections for
parents and children, with a wide range of
interactive learning activities. The parents' section
includes 'Boredom Busters' – a free facility that
searches for attractions and special events within
10–50km of your postcode area.

24 Hour Museum
www.24hourmuseum.org.uk

A guide to over 2,500 museums, galleries and
heritage attractions.

Advisory Centre for Education
www.ace-ed.org.uk

The Advisory Centre for Education (ACE) is an
independent advice centre for parents, providing
information about state education in England and
Wales for 5–16-year-olds. ACE offers free advice
on many topics, including exclusion from school,
bullying, special educational needs and school
admission appeals.

Parentline Plus
www.parentlineplus.org.uk

Parentline Plus offers advice for parents and
carers. Freephone helpline 24 hours a day:
0808 800 2222.

Parents Online
www.parents.org.uk

A website to help parents with children through
their primary school years.

Gingerbread
www.gingerbread.org.uk

Gingerbread brings lone parents together for
mutual support.
Freephone: 0800 018 4318

Raising Kids
www.raisingkids.co.uk

A website with general advice for parents on
raising children.

Mumsnet
www.mumsnet.com

Mumsnet is an online network of parents pooling
their knowledge.

Fathers Direct

www.fathersdirect.com

Fathers Direct is the UK's national information centre for fatherhood. The website designed by fathers for fathers. It contains a lot of information also for professionals working with fathers.

Pink Parents

www.pinkparents.org.uk

A UK-wide charity of, for and by lesbian, gay and bisexual parents, parents-to-be and their children.

Disabled Parents Network

www.disabledparentsnetwork.org.uk
Helpline: 0870 241 0450

National NEWPIN

www.newpin.org.uk

A charity which supports parents under stress and runs local centres which offer long term emotional support to families.
Tel: 020 7358 5900

National Council for One Parent families

www.oneparentfamilies.org.uk
Helpline: 0800 018 5026

Childcare Link

www.childcarelink.gov.uk

A website that enables you to search for local and national childcare information.

Dual language and mother-tongue resources

A range of multilingual and mother-tongue resources and books are available from the following organisations.

Mantralingua
www.mantralingua.com

Milet
www.milet.com

The Refugee Council
www.refugeecouncil.org.uk

Hounslow Language Service
www.ealinhounslow.org.uk

Hounslow Language Service publishes a free leaflet for parents, *Advantages of Being Bilingual*, on the importance of helping children to maintain their first language. The leaflet is currently available in Arabic, Bengali, English, Farsi, Gujarati, Hindi, Punjabi, Somali, Spanish and Urdu.

Learning Design
www.learningdesign.biz

Roy Yates Books
Smallfields Cottage
Cox Green
Rudgwick
Horsham
RH12 3DE
Tel: 01403 822 299

Grant and Cutler
www.grantandcutler.com

Supplementary and mother-tongue schools

The Resource Unit for Supplementary and Mother-Tongue Schools
www.resourceunit.com

The Resource Unit provides advice and support to supplementary and mother-tongue schools. The Resource Unit School Directory provides details of 1,000 supplementary and mother-tongue schools in the UK (www.resourceunit.com/sch_directory/sch_directory.html).

The Resource Unit also publishes *Towards More Effective Supplementary and Mother-tongue Schools* (www.resourceunit.com/effective.htm).

Supplementary Schools Support Service
www.supplementaryschools.org.uk

A national agency that works to build links between schools and their local communities.

4

Providing advice and support to parents

4 Providing advice and support to parents

> "Without help on every matter like housing, benefits and education we would have had great difficulty in managing everyday life."
>
> **Khider, parent from Iraq**

Setting the context

School staff have always been a source of support and advice for parents about issues relating to their children's education. It is widely recognised that providing advice and support to parents will have a positive effect on children's well-being and educational progress.

Parents have increasingly turned to schools, not only as a source of support on issues related to their children, but as a means of support for their own needs and difficulties. They often feel more comfortable talking to school staff they know and trust than they do approaching other, often unfamiliar, agencies.

"Through the pupils, and increasingly from the parents themselves, we became aware of the pressures and problems they faced. Coming to talk about an education issue often opened up the deep underlying concerns of the parent. Parents turned to us for advice and support. The school's concerns were about how to help, while acknowledging the limits of our own experience,

knowledge and expertise. We also recognised the demands that this made on staff, not only in terms of time but also in terms of the personal dilemmas and emotions raised through becoming involved in these personal and family issues. We were the obvious first point of contact."

John Stead, NSPCC Education Programme Co-ordinator and former headteacher, in *Parentaid: A 'how to' guide*, Community Education Development Centre, 2003

Despite increasing pressures on schools, teachers and other staff are usually sympathetic to parents' concerns and try to make time to listen and respond. Many home–school workers and learning mentors have also developed an understanding of wider family needs and have sought to respond positively, often through active advocacy. When welcoming refugee families, schools can build on this existing good practice. Advice and support to refugee families can help promote genuine inclusion and race equality, and will develop skills and expertise that can benefit everyone in the community that the school serves.

Advice and support to refugee and asylum-seeking families

School may be one of the first points of contact for a refugee family. Refugee parents are usually eager for children to attend school as soon as possible because they are aware that this can re-establish daily routines and provide opportunities for children to make friends and learn. School is also one of the few places where families receive a genuine welcome. Inclusive admission and induction procedures mean that schools need to listen to families, identify needs and target extra support. In primary schools, parents are usually on site twice a day and there are many opportunities to establish home–school communication and partnership.

Schools that have taught refugee children for many years are aware that families can have complex needs, which can adversely impact on children's health, well-being and learning. Although schools may have limited resources and cannot be expected to respond to every type of problem, they are well placed to identify potential difficulties and help families find the support they need.

Recent Ofsted guidance recognises the valuable work of schools in responding to the needs of vulnerable families, including refugees, who may arrive during the year. According to Ofsted (2002) these schools:

- forge relationships with parents quickly
- deal efficiently with issues of immediate concern – such as medical conditions, systems of contact, school uniform, free school meals and homework
- develop contacts with other agencies such as housing, social services, education welfare and the voluntary sector.

Signposting

School staff may not, in most cases, have the appropriate knowledge and skills to respond to complex needs. They may be unaware of organisations, services and agencies in the local community that can help families. School staff should not give advice in those areas where they lack expertise – this may do more harm than good. It is also a criminal offence to provide advice on immigration and asylum matters, unless one is registered with, or granted a certificate of exemption by the Office of the Immigration Services Commissioner (OISC).

However, schools could usefully direct families to appropriate sources of support, and also make well-informed referrals. Therefore, it is important that schools find out about local services, make contact with them and assemble information that can be updated on a regular basis.

This approach has been successfully used by Salusbury WORLD and other outreach projects. It has also been piloted by **Parentaid** projects in schools and LEAs across the UK. The **Parentaid** process involves staff in schools, nurseries and childcare settings keeping a record of the family and personal concerns raised with them, auditing support services (community, voluntary and statutory) available to parents in the local community and creating a directory of information for professionals and volunteers working with children, parents and families. There are many benefits to this approach including:

- Schools feel more confident and better equipped to deal with parents' requests for help
- Partnerships are developed between the school and local organisations which can be of benefit to both
- Parents have a local, familiar place where they can gain access to the information and support they need.

Parentaid: School and community working together to support parents, ContinYou, 1999

See page 139 for more information on Parentaid and ContinYou.

What type of advice is available?

In most areas there will be a range of support agencies providing advice and support to all sections of the population, including minority ethnic communities and refugees. Many organisations focus specifically on advising refugees, and it is useful for schools to be aware of who they are and what help they provide. See page 140 for details of a wide range of advice and support organisations that help refugees.

Local organisations and services may provide different kinds of advice. The most common are likely to be the following.

ADVICE SURGERIES

A parent visits the organisation for advice. Many organisations have advice surgeries on particular days of the week. One-to-one support is often provided. Some agencies also provide interpreters for appointments or use telephone interpreting services such as Language Line.

OUTREACH ADVICE

A parent meets an adviser in another setting. This may be at a refugee community organisation, at school or at home. Sometimes outreach workers visit with interpreters.

TELEPHONE ADVICE

Many agencies have telephone advice lines. These are usually available for only part of the week and at designated times.

INFORMATION BOOKLETS

There are leaflets and booklets for refugees covering issues such as the asylum process, housing, benefits, education and health. The Refugee Council and the British Red Cross both provide information which is translated into different languages.

Compiling information on local organisations

A great deal of information about local resources can be obtained by contacting the local CAB or Council for Voluntary Service. When compiling information, a school should try to find out the following:

- the name of the organisation
- the area covered by its services

- the address and telephone number
- opening times
- times for telephone or drop-in advice sessions
- the name of a contact person
- what advice and support they can offer parents
- whether interpreters are provided
- the method of referral.

The pro forma **Local services information template** on page 157 can be used to collect and record information.

Information should be kept in a format that is accessible to staff – a ring binder may be useful. Leaflets and posters can also be collected for display and to give to parents. Some refugee organisations or other statutory and voluntary

services have compiled and printed handbooks of useful information and contacts for refugees. These can be very helpful and informative and are worth obtaining.

The following sections provide more specific information and advice on:
- **immigration and asylum** (page 113)
- **housing** (page 121)
- **health** (page 126)
- **adult education**, **training and employment** (page 131)
- **money and benefits** (page 136).

Each section highlights the main difficulties that refugees experience and sets out strategies and good practice for schools.

Salusbury WORLD and Citizens Advice Bureau partnership

In order to meet the growing demand and complexity of advice work, Salusbury WORLD established a partnership with the local Citizens Advice Bureau (CAB). One of their outreach refugee officers is now based at Salusbury WORLD for half a day a week. He offers half-hourly appointments to clients from the school community and from the community at large, and deals with issues such as immigration, welfare benefits, housing and debt. The service is well used and has the following benefits:

- it reaches people who are unaware of the CAB
- people feel more comfortable in an environment which is already familiar to them

- there is easier access to interpreters, because the volunteer interpreters already working at Salusbury WORLD can be used
- the appointment booking system is easier to access than the CAB advice line.

Immigration and asylum

> "I have been here five years now. I feel very isolated and anxious. There are times when I can't stand it and want the Home Office to make their decision as quickly as possible so that I know what will happen to me for sure and can get on with my life. The waiting is the hardest thing, as you are completely unsure about the future. I feel as if my life depends upon a bit of paper."
>
> **Holta, aged 14, from Kosova**

Asylum-seekers are people who have fled from their home country and have made an application to the Home Office for asylum (a request for protection under the 1951 UN Convention Relating to the Status of Refugees). Applications can be made by individual adults, family units and by separated (unaccompanied) children. Family separation during persecution and flight is common and many families do not arrive in the UK at the same time. Although unusual, there may also be circumstances when it may be appropriate for a child to make an application in their own right.

Asylum procedures are complex and have been affected by frequent changes of legislation. Since 1993, there have been five major pieces of immigration and asylum legislation. The most recent is the Asylum and Immigration (Treatment of Claimants etc.) Act 2004.

Applying for asylum

Asylum applications can be made on arrival at a port of entry (airports and seaports) or after entry ('in-country') at a Home Office Asylum Screening Unit. The main Asylum Screening Units are located in Croydon and Liverpool. Applicants will be asked questions about how they travelled to the UK and will be fingerprinted. They will usually then be issued a plastic identity card – an Application Registration Card (ARC) which is the size of a credit card and includes the asylum applicant's photo and personal details. The ARC confirms that the person has applied for asylum in the UK. The ARC replaces the earlier Standard Acknowledgement Letter (SAL) that used to be issued to new applicants.

The majority of asylum applicants are given Statement of Evidence (SEF) application forms to complete and return within ten working days.

The SEF gives a person an opportunity to state in writing their reasons for applying for asylum. The form is about 19 pages long and very complex. It has to be completed in English with all supporting documents translated into English within the time allocated. Asylum-seekers who do not comply with these requirements may be refused for 'non-compliance' without their case being considered substantively. If they have submitted information, however, that information ought to be considered, but any non-compliance will count against them, either because they do not get the benefit of an interview or because their non-compliance is taken as indicating they do not view their claim as serious.

Asylum decisions and appeals

After the SEF has been returned to the Home Office, asylum-seekers will usually attend a full asylum interview. Often, asylum-seekers will be expected to attend interviews on their own because legal aid is generally not available for representation at interview.

The Home Office has stated that it aims to resolve initial asylum decisions within two months. Following changes in the tribunal appeals system, from April 2005, it is intended that appeals should become even faster – in future appeals may be completed in weeks rather than months. When an asylum-seeker has dependants, the decision given to the principal applicant applies to the whole family. For example, if a child's mother is given full refugee status, this decision applies also to her dependent children.

The UK is a signatory to the 1951 Refugee Convention and has a duty to properly consider all applications made under it. The Refugee Convention defines who is a refugee and entitled to protection. A decision by the Home Office on an asylum application will be one of the following:

Refugee status: If the Home Office accepts that an asylum applicant has a well-founded fear of being persecuted for reasons stated in the 1951 Refugee Convention he or she will be granted Indefinite Leave to Remain (ILR) as a refugee. An asylum-seeker granted ILR has immediate permanent residence in the UK.

Exceptional Leave to Remain (ELR): This status is not granted anymore, but some asylum-seekers may have been granted ELR in the past. For those that still have ELR and will have completed four years by the time ELR expires, they may apply for Indefinite Leave to Remain (ILR) at the end of those four years. Ordinarily this should be granted.

Humanitarian Protection: This is granted where the Home Office recognises that there is a real risk of death, torture, or other inhuman and degrading treatment that falls outside the strict terms of the 1951 Refugee Convention. Those granted Humanitarian Protection will normally be given leave to remain for three years. After this period, their case will be reviewed. This may result in an Extension of Protection, a grant of Discretionary Leave, a grant of Indefinite Leave to Remain or a refusal of leave where the person may be required to leave the UK.

Discretionary Leave: The Home Office will grant Discretionary Leave to someone who does not quality for refugee status or humanitarian protection but cannot be removed. This may be because they have a serious medical condition making travel or return dangerous. Discretionary Leave will normally be granted for a period of three years but can also be granted for shorter periods. Discretionary Leave may be extended, but no application for Indefinite Leave to Remain will be considered before someone has had a period of six years Discretionary Leave.

Refusal: Asylum-seekers may also have their case refused. From April 2005, appeals may be made to the new Asylum and Immigration Tribunal, which will replace the Immigration Appellate Authority and the Immigration Appeals Tribunal. However, there is an increasing chance that asylum-seekers will be refused a right of appeal while they remain in the UK because (a) they come from a particular country which the Home Office presumes to be safe; (b) they have passed through a particular country to which the Home Office says they can be safely returned; or (c) the Home Office says their case is clearly unfounded. The Home Office has also substantially increased its powers to remove asylum-seekers to countries which the Home Office says are safe, even though an asylum-seeker has neither passed through nor has any other connection to that particular country. The Home Office is exploring with other countries ways in which it may use these powers, including setting up refugee camps overseas.

Other decisions: The Home Office has a general discretion over immigration control. Therefore, some asylum-seekers are granted

leave to remain, whether indefinitely or for a fixed period, even if they do not strictly fall within any of the categories set out above, because there are compelling reasons why they should not be expected to return to their home country.

There are Immigration Rules and Home Office policies and concessions related to the length of time people have been in the UK. Some asylum-seekers have been in the UK for so long that one of the following categories apply:

- asylum-seekers who have been in the UK with children for a period of seven years should usually be considered for Indefinite Leave to Remain unless the children are, or are close to becoming, adults
- asylum-seekers who have been in the UK lawfully for ten years should usually be considered for Indefinite Leave to Remain
- asylum-seekers who have been in the UK, lawfully or not, for 14 years should usually be considered for Indefinite Leave to Remain
- asylum-seekers whose asylum claim was made before 1 January 1996 and are still awaiting an initial decision by the Home Office may be entitled to Indefinite Leave to Remain.
- asylum-seekers who claimed before 2 October 2000, and were accompanied by minor dependent children on that date or on 24 October 2003 may also be entitled to Indefinite Leave to Remain for themselves and their families.

Initial interview and application

Asylum-seekers may have to face long interviews just hours after they arrive and before they have a chance to get advice and representation. Being afraid, tired and disorientated may mean that important information is left out.

Most refugees do not know what the Home Office expects of them. They are not aware that they may be expected to provide evidence and documents to support their asylum claim. Others may be too traumatised to give a full account of what has happened to them. For example, women may not mention shameful forms of abuse such as rape in their asylum interview, particularly if the interviewer or interpreter is male. Others may have been given strict instructions as to what they should say, and are frightened that they may be returned straightaway if they do not follow this advice. The Home Office may hold errors or omissions against the asylum-seeker when it makes a decision.

Accessing information

Many asylum-seekers have little information about the asylum process in the UK and what their rights and entitlements are. The Refugee Council produces translated information on a range of topics (www.refugeecouncil.org.uk/ publications).

Legal advice and representation

It is vital that an asylum-seeker finds a legal representative to help with his or her asylum claim. Asylum applications are complicated and a good representative may be able to help someone who is being refused unfairly.

A legal representative can be a solicitor, barrister, caseworker from a specialist agency such as the Refugee Legal Centre or Asylum Aid, or someone from a refugee organisation. Representatives who are not regulated by their own professional body, as are solicitors or barristers, are legally bound to register with the Office of the Immigration Services Commissioner (OISC). The OISC regulates the provision of legal advice and representation, and persons not exempted or registered to give advice may be prosecuted.

Asylum support

As asylum-seekers are not allowed to work they will need to be supported while they go through the asylum process. They may be able to apply for support from the National Asylum Support Service (NASS). NASS is the government department responsible for supporting destitute asylum-seekers. Support from NASS means an asylum applicant can get help with accommodation and help with living expenses (cash support). Asylum-seekers who wish to stay with friends and relatives may choose to apply only for cash support.

Previously, a family or 'household' with children under 18 should not have been refused support from NASS in any circumstances. However, recently introduced powers mean that families whose claims and appeals have been finally rejected may be refused housing and support. Any family faced with this predicament will need urgent legal advice.

Agencies such as the Refugee Council, Refugee Action, the Refugee Arrivals Project, Migrant Helpline, the Scottish Refugee Council and the Welsh Refugee Council provide advice and information on accommodation and cash support. Local advice organisations such as Citizens Advice Bureaux may also offer support. See **General advice for refugees** on page 140 for details of organisations that offer help and advice.

Family separation and reunion

Most asylum-seekers experience some form of loss and separation from home and family when they flee. Children may be separated from one or both of their parents for long periods.

It may be a long time before families can be reunited. Once an asylum-seeker is granted refugee status, he or she is entitled to apply for family reunion. Family reunion for refugees is not subject to the strict requirements that apply to others who wish their families to join them. People granted Indefinite Leave to Remain in the UK for reasons other than asylum may apply for their family to join them but will have to satisfy various requirements that they can maintain their family. There may be exceptional circumstances where asylum-seekers granted other statuses can also make such applications.

Schools should be aware that family separations may impact on the health and development of children and should offer support when appropriate.

Waiting for decisions

Despite the government's attempts to speed up the decision-making process on claims, asylum-seekers may have to wait a long time to get a final decision, especially if they go through the appeals process. Not knowing the outcome of a claim can lead to a strong sense of insecurity for families and can affect their ability to settle. This time can be particularly difficult, as the Home Office is not consistent as to how long it takes, or which cases take longer than others. Sometimes, therefore, an asylum-seeker may feel particularly distressed because they know of others in the community, or even their own family, who have received decisions much more quickly.

Refusals and appeals

Receiving a negative decision from the Home Office can be very upsetting for families. Often asylum-seekers receive very long letters refusing them asylum. The letter may be confusing or contain serious errors. Sometimes an asylum-seeker is refused despite knowing that another person from their community or family has been granted status. This can be confusing and distressing. Going through an appeals process, coupled with the fear of being sent back to the country of origin, can be very stressful and cause great anxiety to parents and children.

Many schools and teachers are concerned at the increasing numbers of families receiving notification that they are going to be removed or deported from the UK. Their children may be settled in school and have made friends and may be progressing in their learning. Some schools and local communities actively campaign against removals and deportations, and have been successful.

More information on school anti-deportation campaigns can be found at:
- **Schools Against Deportations:** www.irr.org.uk/sad
- **National Coalition of Anti-Deportation Campaigns:** www.ncadc.org.uk.

Family or private life in the UK

Asylum-seekers may have established a new life for themselves here, particularly if their claim or appeal has been subject to lengthy delays. This may include getting married and having children. Where the delay is particularly long, or the possibility of the family relocating is particularly difficult, this may provide a reason to challenge a Home Office decision to return the asylum-seeker. However, in marriage cases, the Home Office and immigration courts will always consider whether or not it is reasonable to expect an asylum-seeker to return to their home country and apply to join their spouse from there, as others seeking to immigrate to the UK for marriage will have to do.

Separated and unaccompanied refugee and asylum-seeking children

Separated asylum-seeking children
Children under 18 years of age who are outside their country of origin and separated from both parents or their legal/customary primary care giver.

Unaccompanied asylum-seeking children
Children under 18 years of age who are outside their country of origin and not accompanied by a close relative.
> *Cold Comfort: Young separated refugees in England*, Save the Children (2001)

Children who arrive in the UK on their own should be supported by social services. Usually they will be granted Discretionary Leave to Remain in the UK until their 18th birthday, unless the Home Office is able to ensure that the child will be suitably looked after if returned to their home country.

Children's cases can be very difficult. Young people's ages are often disputed by the Home Office or social services. It is often difficult to assess a person's age because they may arrive without identification documents or with false documents. Age disputes are often about whether the young person is under or over 18 years of age.

Asylum-seeking children and young people do not have an automatic right to be reunited with their parents or family members in the UK. A child may apply to the Home Office for their relatives to be allowed to enter the UK on compassionate grounds, but permission will not necessarily be granted.

Another difficult time is when the child is about to turn 18. At this time, not only their status may be coming to an end, but their eligibility for support from social services may be about to cease also.

Good practice in school

Schools should be aware that families and children might be coping with stress and uncertainty during the asylum process. A genuine welcome to school, along with good communication and effective admission and induction procedures will provide reassurance to families.

Hostile media coverage of asylum issues and widespread prejudice may mean that families are wary of talking about their immigration situation. They may also worry that what they say might not be kept confidential, or that schools may share information with the Home Office. It may be necessary to assure families that schools are concerned with the best interests and well-being of children and have no links with the immigration authorities or any responsibility to divulge information to them.

Schools can gain an awareness of the organisations and agencies that provide good quality advice to asylum-seekers. There may also be cases when schools and legal representatives work together to support children and families.

How schools can help – a checklist

✓ Be aware of how prejudice and racism against asylum-seekers may impact on the well-being and safety of children and families. Schools should ensure that all staff receive training so that myths and wrong information about asylum-seekers can be challenged.

✓ Provide information to families on where they can get advice and support on asylum and immigration matters.

✓ Display translated information booklets for asylum-seekers and people with refugee status, humanitarian protection or discretionary leave.

✓ Ensure that separated refugee and asylum-seeking children (often described as unaccompanied children) have appropriate legal advice. Joint working between schools and other professionals will be essential for ensuring that separated children receive appropriate support and access their entitlements.

✓ Help families understand letters they might receive from the Home Office and make sure they know that their legal representatives can provide interpreters for them.

✓ Write letters of support and make representations when requested by families and legal representatives. When writing letters it is always vital to liaise with legal representatives first. Sometimes letters can be very useful, but at other times their use is lost because the writer has undermined their good points by commenting upon something they are not qualified to comment upon (eg, the situation in the asylum-seeker's home country).

Case study

Abdul, aged 8, arrived from Somalia in the UK in 1998 with his elder sister, her husband and their baby. Abdul had lived in a refugee camp in Kenya for many months after fleeing Somalia with his parents and siblings before he came to the UK. He had received very little formal education either in Somalia or Kenya and since he was born he had experienced only disruption in his life.

Abdul was disoriented and took a long time to settle at school. He had little ability to concentrate, was disruptive in class and found it difficult to make meaningful friendships.

Abdul was found to have special educational needs and received learning support which slowly helped his educational progress but his behaviour did not improve significantly. When a Somali education worker talked to him in Somali it was clear that Abdul was very upset and angry with his parents for not being in the UK with him. Abdul would often ask if the school could make his parents come over.

Salusbury WORLD referred Abdul and his sister to a reputable immigration solicitor who applied for a family reunion on compassionate grounds. However, during this process Abdul's father and brother unexpectedly arrived in UK and were accommodated in a bed and breakfast hotel while their asylum application was being considered. After several weeks the Home Office decided to disperse them to new accommodation outside London. For Abdul, staying with his father would therefore have meant leaving Salusbury Primary School and more instability.

Salusbury WORLD collected letters of support from Abdul's class teacher, the Headteacher, the learning support teacher and the SENCO to argue for the newly-reunited family to stay in London. These letters were faxed to NASS (the National Asylum Support Service) with a successful outcome. Abdul's father was provided with accommodation in London. Abdul was able to be with him and continue attending Salusbury Primary.

Housing

"I don't like living in the hotel because it smells. When we come in and it's raining outside there is nowhere to put our wet clothes. There is nowhere to do my homework, so I do it on my bed. It's noisy because my little brother and sisters are playing. It's small and difficult to sleep because we all sleep in the same room. There are people shouting at night. We can't have people to visit so my friends can't come and play. The toilet is in the bathroom and it smells. Lots of people use the kitchen and it's too small and it's difficult to do the cooking for our family. We have to put the rubbish bin in our bedroom. It smells and my brother keeps bumping into it. We can't hear the TV because it is too noisy outside."

Halima, 10, from Iraq

Refugees face homelessness and particular difficulties in getting accommodation. Changes in legislation in recent years have restricted the rights of asylum-seekers (people waiting for a decision from the Home Office) to housing, welfare benefits and employment. The Immigration and Asylum Act 1999 introduced sweeping changes to the way asylum-seekers are housed and supported while they wait for a decision on their application. The Home Office set up a new department called the National Asylum Support Service (NASS) responsible for providing accommodation and support.

Some refugees are able to organise their own accommodation but most will need help to get a roof over their heads. The law restricts the rights of asylum-seekers to get help from local housing authorities if they are homeless: they are expected to apply to NASS. Once asylum-seekers have refugee status, humanitarian protection or discretionary leave, they can apply for emergency housing from the local council and go on to the housing waiting list.

Since April 2001, unless there are exceptional circumstances, asylum-seekers are generally dispersed by NASS to accommodation outside London and the south-east, while they await a decision on their asylum claim. NASS is instructed to ignore the wishes of asylum-seekers about where they want to be accommodated or what type of housing they want. They do, however, have to take account of their needs. These needs may include the need to stay close to treatment facilities or support, or to family members, or to stay in a school that is catering well for special needs. They will also not move a family away from an area where a child has started the final year of their GCSEs, AS or A levels, if the child has spent a "significant part" of the previous year in a school or college, and as long as the dispersal has not been delayed because the family was "unco-operative".

Some organisations, like Refugee Action, are funded by the Home Office to support asylum-seekers in NASS accommodation. They may build up local networks of organisations able and willing to help and support asylum-seekers in each area, and may also have volunteers and others who can befriend new arrivals.

Unaccompanied asylum-seeking children are generally housed by social services, and they may also be placed in hostels, bed and breakfast hotels or other temporary housing.

Once an asylum-seeker gets refugee status, humanitarian protection or discretionary leave, she/he can apply for help as homeless, and may do so in whatever area of the country she/he wants to live. If she/he is "in priority need" (for example, because there is a child in the household) she/he will be offered temporary housing and the application assessed. However, if the family has no "local connection" with the area where they have applied for help as homeless, then the local authority can refer them back to an area where they have such a connection. The connection is established by having a job in the area, having close family members who have lived in the area for five years, living in the area (not in NASS accommodation) for six months in the previous year, or because the area is the last place in which

the applicant was housed by NASS (unless it was an accommodation centre or in Scotland).

The main difficulties experienced by asylum-seekers are as follows.

POOR HOUSING CONDITIONS AND OVERCROWDING
Research from the housing charity Shelter (2001) has shown that much of the housing occupied by asylum-seekers is substandard and poses risks to children's health and well-being. In a survey of 154 privately rented dwellings Shelter found:

- nearly 20 per cent were unfit for human habitation
- 19 per cent were infested with cockroaches, fleas and bedbugs
- over 80 per cent of multiple occupancies were exposed to unacceptable risks of fire, many with inadequate means of escape.

Temporary housing is not outside the law, and environmental health officers must inspect housing if they are told it is dangerous to health or safety.

Some refugees living in London and the south-east may choose to receive 'support only' (help with essential living expenses) from NASS and decline to be dispersed to accommodation in other parts of the UK. These families often choose to stay with friends and relatives and may live in very overcrowded accommodation.

BED AND BREAKFAST HOTELS
Refugee children in bed and breakfast hotels may have to share rooms with their parents. It is not uncommon for families to occupy a single room. Families must often share kitchen facilities or may have nowhere to cook at all. Children usually

Excerpt from child's writing

"I'm now 13 and have been living in that crowded, unhygienic room for over three years. The room is on the 4th floor with a winding staircase, long and tiring. The room consists of a double bed, a single bed and a bunk bed, a cupboard and a small fridge and sink. Joined to the room is a toilet and bathroom. The kitchen is shared between four or five families. Cooking is a challenge as there may be no stoves free and other people's mess is left there. I feel ashamed to tell people where I live.

"It is very difficult to do my homework, as the room has no table or chairs so we have to write on the beds, leaning on a book. This is most uncomfortable and can be very tiring when you are doing a long piece of work and bending down all the time. At first I thought this would be temporary but the days, weeks, months, whole years passed and we were still there. A B&B is a place you stay for a short while but this was becoming home.

"I feel like a prisoner, locked in a cage with nowhere to go. As you get older you get more homework which is hard because I have been forced to work in a room where we sleep, eat and drink. I feel like I'm working in the middle of a crowded city where silence rarely exists. I cannot bear it at times, so much that I want to give up. Each time I revised for my SATS in Year 6, the TV was on. It is hard to revise when you have to think over the voice of a giant.

"The room has also meant that all family members have no 'personal space'. I can't even talk to my mum. Sometimes I don't anyway because my parents are so stressed and anxious that I feel it inappropriate to put more weight on them. This means I hold things in which are sometimes too much. I have to let these subdued feelings out, often through crying when I go to sleep."

Ardita, 13, from Albania

have no space to play and or to do homework. They may also lack basic furniture such as a table and chair.

TEMPORARY ACCOMMODATION

Living in temporary accommodation usually means a family has to move frequently and children's education will be disrupted. Families may be re-housed with little prior notice and without regard for children's schooling. Even families who are entitled to permanent housing may have to wait for a long time due to long waiting lists and the priority system.

NASS ACCOMMODATION

Some families are accommodated temporarily by the National Asylum Support Service (NASS), in hostels and bed and breakfast hotels and accommodation before dispersal to another part of the UK. Although this is meant to be for a limited period of time, in reality some families may stay there for weeks or months. While in this 'emergency accommodation', families may be discouraged from putting children into school or registering with doctors. They may also not get the full rate of asylum support.

LOCATION

Families are sometimes accommodated in areas where they may face hostility and racism and be isolated from people who share their language and culture.

LANGUAGE AND BUREAUCRACY

Families often experience tremendous frustration with the bureaucracy of housing departments.

They may not understand how the system works nor access important information or attend vital appointments. Without interpreters or translations some refugees will experience difficulty understanding letters from their housing provider and communicating with housing officials.

MOVING ON WHEN THE ASYLUM APPLICATION IS DECIDED

NASS is meant to give 28 days' notice to families to leave their accommodation when they get refugee status or exceptional leave. In practice it is often a lot less. Families are then meant to get a National Insurance number so they can get social security benefits and find new housing. They have to make crucial decisions, for example about where to apply for help as homeless. What should be a time to celebrate is often a time of additional, sometimes unbearable stress.

STRESS

Overcrowding, poor housing and uncertainty all contribute to stress within families. Stress will affect families in different ways. Some families may be resilient in the face of multiple pressures; others may experience more serious difficulties including mental health problems, changes in parental roles, communication problems and marital/relationship breakdown.

There may also be a greater risk of domestic violence if families occupy unsuitable accommodation for long periods. This may include violent behaviour between parents and between parents and children.

Good practice in school

Schools should be aware how housing issues can affect well-being and be aware of local advice and support for families. In some cases, schools and housing agencies will wish to work together to address issues and problems that are closely related.

How schools can help – a checklist
✓ Keep details of the local asylum-seeker support agency.
✓ See **General advice for refugees** (page 140) for information on agencies that help asylum-seekers get support.
✓ Provide information to families on where they can get advice and support.
✓ Provide facilities to do homework at school.
✓ Write letters for families to use when housing decisions or provision adversely affect children's education and well-being.
✓ Help families understand any letters they receive about their housing.
✓ Advise parents that they are entitled to ask for interpreters for housing appointments.
✓ Ensure that families in temporary accommodation access essential local facilities.
✓ Encourage refugees to join local groups to voice their own concerns.

Case study

A 10 year-old pupil at Salusbury Primary School has lived for the past two years in four different hotels. He shares a room with his mother and father. His mother is being helped by the Medical Foundation for the Care of Victims of Torture and also receives treatment at the local hospital. His father is the mother's carer and also provides most of the parental support. The pupil has now attended four different schools and there are ongoing concerns about his progress, including inappropriate behaviour. Every time that he has settled at a school and started to make friends and progress with his learning, the family has been re-housed.

Salusbury WORLD liaised with the class teacher and together they wrote a letter of support to the local housing department requesting that the family be given their own accommodation near the school. Supporting evidence from the Medical Foundation and local hospital was included with the letter.

The school also made a referral to a charity, The Place to Be (P2B), that provides emotional and therapeutic support to children within the primary school environment.

The housing department considered the evidence from the school and offered the family a flat in a part of the borough where they had a support network. The child was able to continue attending Salusbury Primary School.

Health

> "First it was difficult for me about our health. After one or two months, my husband had asthma and collapsed at the school. Everybody was very kind and helped me. And now my son doesn't need his medicine. Now we are just careful with his food, and we make sure that he is relaxed at night. He used to have medicine and injections in Iran."
>
> **Zahra, parent from Iraq**

All those with a positive decision on their asylum claim and asylum-seekers awaiting a decision on a claim or an appeal are entitled to all NHS care without payment. This includes medical treatment, dental treatment, sight tests, family planning services and prescriptions.

In 2004 significant changes were made to the eligibility of unsuccessful asylum-seekers at the end of the asylum process to NHS care. If a person has been in the UK for more than one year when refused, new hospital care is chargeable, but treatment already underway will be free. If a person has been in the UK for less than one year when refused, all hospital care is chargeable, even if already underway. There are certain exemptions including TB treatment, sexually transmitted infections and HIV counselling and testing, but not HIV treatment. Decisions are currently being made on whether their access to free primary care (GPs and other community health workers) will also be restricted.

Asylum-seekers supported by NASS are issued with a six-month (renewable) HC2 full exemption certificate on behalf of the Department of Health, which exempts the holder from having to pay standard NHS charges. Refugees, people with Humanitarian Protection, Discretionary Leave or Exceptional Leave to Remain and asylum-seekers on a low income can complete an HC1 form and send it to the Health Benefits Division. HC1 forms are available from benefit agency offices, NHS hospitals, doctor's surgeries, or from the Health Benefits Division, Sandyford House, Newcastle-upon-Tyne, NE2 1DB. Tel: 0191 203 5555. They will then receive a HC2 certificate valid for six months after which a new application must be made.

Refugees may experience problems with their health in the UK as well as barriers to receiving appropriate treatment and care. Certain health problems are common among refugees and some are specific to them. Many threats to good health are shared with other deprived and excluded groups, such as problems linked to poverty and overcrowding. Some of the health problems of refugees may be related to human rights abuses in their countries of origin, such as torture. For some refugees, it may take time to pinpoint underlying problems.

Main difficulties

Knowing rights and accessing information
Healthcare systems differ around the world and refugees are often not familiar with health practices in the UK. Refugees may not know whom to see, where to go or if they need to pay for healthcare or medicines. They may be unfamiliar with referral systems and waiting lists, and may not understand letters from doctors or hospitals. Some people may also be embarrassed to ask for help with health problems.

Trust and confidentiality
Some refugee communities may not have had good access to healthcare services in their own country, due to disruption by conflict or for gender reasons. For example, under the rule of the Taliban in Afghanistan, women could not be treated by male doctors and women doctors were not allowed to work. Some refugees may view health workers with mistrust; it may take time to build trust and assure confidentiality.

Interpreting
People may have fears about interpreters maintaining confidentiality, particularly in small communities. For this reason, interpreting for patients at the GP surgery or hospital is often done by family members, including children and friends. This may be problematic, however, as they may not have adequate medical knowledge or language. It also may be inappropriate if there are confidential or embarrassing issues particularly in the areas of sexual health, gynaecological problems, family relationships, domestic violence, child protection, sexual violence or torture. If children interpret for parents, apart from missing school, they also may carry the burden of being exposed to sensitive and private issues.

Finding GPs
Many refugees and asylum-seekers live in temporary accommodation and move frequently, which makes accessing health services and continuity of care more difficult. Some surgeries may also refuse to place them on GP lists if they are full. Under the Race Relations Act, health services cannot discriminate on racial grounds. NHS Direct and local health authority 'Find a Doctor' services can often help with advice when this happens. Some areas also have Primary Care Walk-In Centres that provide healthcare to refugees and other groups that may change accommodation frequently.

Cultural, religious or dietary needs
How, when and what people present to health workers will be influenced by culture and beliefs. It is therefore important to discuss and understand a person's own values and wishes. Cultural, religious and dietary needs of refugees should be understood and addressed. It is also important to be aware that mental illness carries a

stigma in many cultures, which may deter people from seeking help. Many refugees will welcome being able to choose the gender of health workers and interpreters.

Torture and violence

Many asylum-seekers and refugees in the UK have experienced torture and violence. Survivors of torture may not volunteer their history due to feelings of guilt, shame or mistrust. Some children may have experienced torture themselves or have witnessed others being tortured. Many female, and some male, refugees are survivors of sexual violence, including rape.

Much can be done by health workers to alleviate the physical and psychological difficulties that face survivors. In Britain, the Medical Foundation for the Care of Victims of Torture is the main organisation that provides care and rehabilitation to survivors of torture and other forms of organised violence.

Health of women and girls

The particular health difficulties that affect refugee women are often not acknowledged. The needs of women may not be identified, especially in cultures where men are traditionally the spokespeople. Screening and health promotion have tended to have a low uptake among refugee women, but has been improved with an increase in the availability of female health workers and advocates.

Some refugee women and girls may have undergone female genital mutilation (FGM), which can affect sexual health and childbirth. FGM is a criminal offence in the UK under the Prohibition of Female Circumcision Act of 1985 and it is also unlawful to take girls abroad for genital mutilation.

Schools should be aware of child protection issues. If schools have concerns about this issue they should record them, discuss them with social services and seek advice from a specialist agency such as the Foundation for Women's Research and Development (FORWARD) (see page 151 for contact details).

Oral health

Refugees and asylum-seekers may be at risk of poor oral health, reflecting possible limited access to dentists in countries of origin or the conditions of migration. Refugees and asylum-seekers can register with any NHS dentist providing they have an HC2 exemption certificate or Income Support book. If NHS treatment is unavailable from a dentist, the local community dental service will provide help. Community dental services are listed in the telephone directory.

Family stress

Coping with dislocation, family separation, overcrowding and poor housing may place families under considerable stress. Sometimes refugee parents may be struggling with their own needs and this may affect their ability to parent children effectively. Multidisciplinary working between the GP, the health visitor, the school nurse, social services and family centres can ensure an holistic approach when dealing with family problems.

Special education needs

Schools should be wary of making hasty judgements about children's learning and emotional needs. The lack of knowledge of a child's history and communication difficulties may mean that needs are assessed inaccurately. Schools may find it difficult to identify refugee children with special educational needs. Careful monitoring and assessment, supported by good communication with parents can help schools identify difficulties and plan appropriate support. Assessments in a child's first language, with the support of an interpreter, can also be helpful.

The information above was drawn from *Meeting the health needs of refugees and asylum-seekers in the UK: An information and resource pack for health workers* by Angela Burnett and Yohannes Fassil, NHS/Department of Health (2002) http://www.london.nhs.uk/newsmedia/ publications/Asylum_Refugee.pdf

Good practice in school

There is much that schools can do to ensure children and families receive support with health needs. Indeed, school is often the first place where problems and difficulties may be noticed. On entry, families are asked about health needs and schools should check whether they are registered with a GP. Schools are well placed to liaise with local health services to increase the possibility of health needs being addressed.

How schools can help with health needs – a checklist
The following are some of the ways that schools can help with health needs. Building up an awareness of local agencies and services can

enable appropriate referrals to be made. See **Health advice** on page 150 for sources of information.

✓ Raise awareness of the particular health needs of refugee children and families.

✓ Be aware that health problems may be linked with other concerns such as housing, money and immigration problems.

✓ Ensure each new child has a health check by school nurse/school health adviser on entry to the school and that appropriate referrals are made if necessary. If your school doesn't have a school nurse, be clear about what alternative services are available.

✓ Provide information about healthcare in the UK, including translated information if available.

✓ Ensure that children living in local hotels access school places quickly.

✓ Write letters on behalf of children and families.

✓ Ensure that parents know interpreters and health advocates are available in the NHS.

✓ Help set up appointments if necessary.

✓ Provide information about health projects and services in the local area. Leaflets and translated information could be made available in school.

✓ Find out about health outreach services for homeless families, including those in bed and breakfast hotels.

✓ Work in partnership with local health services, taking a multi-agency approach.

✓ Ensure pre-school children have access to early years services.

✓ Talk about health issues with children and establish good nutrition and hygiene habits.

Case study

When a 6-year-old Iranian boy was admitted to Salusbury Primary, the parents informed staff that the child had severe medical problems. Neither parent spoke English; one spoke Farsi and the other spoke Arabic and a little Farsi. The parents showed a staff member the medicine from Iran and indicated that the child's development was impaired in some way. The father asked to be informed if the child was bullied by other children.

The family were immediately referred to the school nurse, who booked a Farsi interpreter for the appointment, which unfortunately was cancelled at short notice. The school had built up contacts with other parents and was able to call on a Farsi-speaking doctor who used to have a child at the school. He was able to come in at short notice and establish the type of medication brought from Iran and what it was being used for. He explained that it was to treat epilepsy but was not medication licensed for use in the UK. He also found out that the child was suffering from a severe developmental delay caused by oxygen starvation to the brain that had occurred in the child's infancy.

With this information, the school nurse was able to make several immediate referrals, including one to the school doctor. The teacher was informed of the boy's condition and was made aware that because of the epilepsy, he should take extra care with PE and with getting cold, both of which could trigger an attack.

The school doctor advised the parents to discontinue the Iranian medicine immediately. He also referred the child to the speech and language therapy service and to the epilepsy department of the local hospital.

The parents were reassured that the child was not being bullied and that the class teacher had encouraged children in the class to welcome and befriend him. However, it was clear that sometimes he annoyed other children by being over-affectionate and kissing their faces or hugging them. His father said he would encourage him not to do this. The child now receives support at school with his learning needs.

Adult education, training and employment

"Salusbury WORLD ran a three-week intensive course in Basic English for refugee parents. One of the teachers showed us details about other courses we could try. I picked a one-year course in Library Assistance – I really enjoyed it. Salusbury WORLD helped me find two weeks' voluntary work in a library so I could have some practice instead of just theory – it was a great experience. I have to say Salusbury WORLD has helped me and my family with everything. They were fantastic, very helpful. What can I say? They changed my life; I wouldn't have survived in the UK without them."

Dhurata, parent from Kosova

Refugees and asylum-seekers may have different needs when it comes to education, training and employment. This is due to the fact that they come to UK with diverse educational and professional backgrounds, ranging from those who are highly qualified and have had years of experience in their chosen profession, to those who may not have had access to any education or training. In the case of asylum-seekers, a key barrier to education is their immigration status, which means they cannot access government-funded training schemes and statutory student support for higher education.

When it comes to employment, the barriers are even greater. Despite the significant skills gap in the UK, many refugees find it difficult to gain employment due to their unfamiliarity with employment rights, their lack of work experience in the UK, the absence of references from this country, employers' discrimination and their lack of fluency in English. Furthermore, since July 2002, newly arriving asylum-seekers are banned from working.

Given the opportunity to work, refugees make significant contributions to the UK economy. Recent research by the Learning and Skills Council showed that 66 per cent of those asylum-seekers and refugees who were employed in their countries of origin were engaged in skilled or professional work and 20 per cent had degrees.[1] According to a BBC Scotland documentary broadcast in May 2003, three-quarters of refugees living in Scotland are qualified to do highly skilled jobs.

Having unemployed parents means that refugee children are more likely to live in poverty and be unable to participate in activities that cost money. This may affect children's achievement in school and have a wider negative impact on well-being, health and family life.

Main difficulties

Learning English

Many refugees urgently need to learn English. Not having basic English can increase the feeling of isolation and can be a major barrier to accessing services. For those who wish to access education or employment, not having a good level of English represents one of the key barriers they have to overcome.

There are many English language classes available to refugees. However, the demand for places is high and they are often full. Some organisations and colleges run free English classes for refugees and may also provide help with transport and childcare. There are different levels and types of English language courses in the UK. They include:

- **ESOL (English for Speakers of Other Languages)** courses are general English classes and are available from beginner to advanced levels. They focus on the English that refugees and asylum-seekers need to use in everyday situations, plus basic grammar. These courses can lead to qualifications, such as Pitman, RSA, University of Cambridge Local Examinations Syndicate (UCLES). ESOL can also be offered with other subjects such as Information Technology.

- **English for academic purposes** is suitable for those who want to go on to higher education and study in a particular subject area.
- **English for specific purposes** is taught to a group of people in a specific field of work and it covers the English needed in vocational areas, such as catering, engineering, medicine or law.
- **EFL (English as a Foreign Language)** courses very from beginner to proficiency level and are suitable for overseas students, but may also be useful for refugees. The fee for these courses is usually high.

Further education colleges, adult education centres and some other training providers can be contacted for more information on the above courses.

Work ban on asylum-seekers

On the 23rd of July 2002, the Government withdrew the concession allowing asylum-seekers to apply for permission to work if they had been waiting for a decision on their asylum claim for six months or more. Asylum-seekers are no longer able to work or undertake vocational training until they are given a positive decision on their asylum case, regardless of how long they have to wait for a decision. However, the Home Office can grant permission for asylum-seekers to work if they have been waiting for a decision on their asylum claim for 12 months. However, this is only done in exceptional circumstances.

If an asylum-seeker was granted permission to work before 23rd July 2002, but his/her asylum claim has since been refused, he/she can continue to work whilst waiting for the outcome of an appeal.

Asylum-seekers without permission to work are entitled to do voluntary work, which gives them a chance to gain some work experience. The organisation they are volunteering for will normally provide meals and travel expenses.

Anyone with refugee status or Humanitarian Protection, Discretionary Leave or Exceptional Leave to Remain has the right to work in the UK. They do not need to tell the Home Office before applying for or taking up a job.

Accessing information

One of the key barriers to education and employment is the lack of information and advice services across UK to help refugees and asylum-seekers make informed choices about their education, training and employment needs. Because many refugees are unfamiliar with the UK system, they may need information, support and advice to find out about employment rights, jobs, ESOL and college courses. They may also need advice when completing application forms and preparing for interviews. Organisations such as Refugee Education and Training Advisory Service (RETAS, a division of Education Action International), the Refugee Assessment and Guidance Unit (RAGU) and the Refugee Council provide such help

Discrimination

Many refugees experience discrimination when they apply for jobs. Refugee organisations have also said that employers do not always value experiences, skills and qualifications gained overseas. Some employment sectors, such voluntary and public sector, follow the Equal Opportunities policy in recruitment and these

sectors may offer more employment opportunities for refugees.

Recognition of qualifications

Non-British qualifications may not be accepted in the UK. Refugees may arrive without documentary evidence of study and qualifications gained in their home country. Although refugees may not need to completely retrain, they may have to do a conversion course for recognition or to become familiar with UK working practices. Refugees should be referred to specialist advice about their qualifications and professional experience. Along with RETAS, RAGU and the Refugee Council, the UK National Academic Recognition Information Centre (UK NARIC) provides this kind of help. This service is not free if a refugee approaches them directly, but RETAS can approach UK NARIC on behalf of a client, in which case the service is free of charge.

Access to further and higher education

There are many reasons why refugees or asylum-seekers may want to further their education. Common ones include:
- gaining or improving English language skills
- acquiring new skills and knowledge
- completing an interrupted course of education
- topping up unrecognised academic qualifications
- gaining a British qualification
- re-qualifying in their profession
- socialising and being less isolated.

There are no legal restrictions preventing refugees from studying at any level of further or higher education. All categories of refugees, including asylum-seekers, who are in receipt of state benefits, including assistance from the NASS, are eligible for Learning and Skills Council funding, which entitles them to nil fees or remission of fees. Entitlements to Learner Support Funds in further education, which are available for students in need, will depend on age and asylum status.

When it comes to higher education, refugees with refugee status, ELR, HP or DL are entitled to pay home student fees, while asylum-seekers can legally be charged overseas fees. Asylum-seekers are not eligible for statutory student support. People with ELR, HP or DL, need to fulfil the 'three years ordinary residence' criteria before the start of the course. Those with refugee status are eligible from the date their status was granted. Asylum-seekers without permission to work are no longer eligible for government-funded training programmes including New Deal or work-based training schemes. Those with refugee status, ELR, HP or DL are eligible.

The organisations mentioned above will provide more detailed advice on all areas covered in this section. Libraries also have information about local courses.

Education and training needs of refugee women
Refugee women sometimes need special help to find education and employment opportunities. Some cultures prefer single-sex classes and women teachers. Also, women often have the main responsibility for childcare and will need affordable crèche facilities. There are several organisations that assist refugee women, including:
- The Refugee Council Training and Education Service
- Education Action International
- Refugee Women's Association
- African Refugee Women's Access to Education and Training Project.

Some of these organisations also run outreach provision including home visits.

See **Education, training and employment advice** on page 152 for details of where refugee women can get advice with education needs.

Good practice in school

Refugees' entitlements to education are governed by complex laws, regulations, rulings and funding councils' decisions, which are also subject to constant change. Professional advice and guidance, therefore, should always be sought.

Refugee parents may approach their child's school for advice about employment and education. Schools can play an important role by providing information about sources of advice and support. See **Education, training and employment advice** on page 152 for lists of agencies that can provide specialised advice in this area.

How schools can help parents with adult education, training and employment needs – a checklist
✓ Find out who provides ESOL courses locally, where they take place and how to enrol.
✓ Establish links with local community organisations and adult education colleges. Most will have prospectuses and other information that you can make available in school.

✓ Ensure that refugee parents have information about classroom assistant, teaching assistant and learning mentor posts in the school. These have proved to be an important route into part-time and full-time employment for many parents.

✓ Ensure that refugee parents know about opportunities for volunteering. Refugees are permitted to work as volunteers as soon as they apply for asylum. Through volunteering, refugees can meet other people, improve their English and get UK work experience that is vital when applying for a paid job.

✓ Volunteering opportunities can be found in local libraries, local newspapers, local charities and voluntary organisations. See **Volunteers** on page 83 for information on organisations that connect people to volunteering opportunities.

✓ Provide opportunities for parents to access computers and the Internet, which may be essential for job searching.

✓ Write references for parents if they have volunteered in school.

✓ Direct parents to the local Job Centre, which may have information about programmes aimed at getting refugee communities into to work.

✓ Consider joint initiatives with colleges and other adult education providers – eg, inviting them to school to explain opportunities.

✓ Look for free or affordable childcare provision which may be available for parents.

✓ Direct parents to specialist advice and guidance on access to further and higher education. See **Education, training and employment advice** on page 152 for details of where refugee women can get advice with education needs.

Providing education advice to parents at Salusbury WORLD

Many parents attending Salusbury WORLD for advice and support felt frustrated and discouraged because they were not confident in English. Many parents who wanted to enrol for ESOL and other courses and training had no access to affordable childcare.

Salusbury WORLD found that ESOL, Personal & Professional Development and IT programmes were provided free by the Brent Adult and Community Education Service (BACES), in numerous centres, many within walking distance. Some of the centres also offered free or discounted crèche facilities. Contact was established with BACES and many parents were referred to them.

Representatives from BACES were also invited to Salusbury WORLD to meet families and provide information about ESOL courses. Interpreters were provided.

This initiative resulted in many more parents enrolling in ESOL courses. Consequently they became more confident communicating with teachers and dealing with housing and benefits matters.

Money and benefits

"In my country I had my own business manufacturing fabrics. I want to set up in this country but I don't know how your system works, or what people in this country like. I have spent a lot of money travelling all over, to Manchester and Bradford and many places to get a job, but no one has even answered me. So I live on benefits. But it makes me sad. Children look up to their father; he should set an example to them. What dreams can my children have for their future if they see their father on benefit?"

Wasel, parent from Syria.

Most asylum-seekers are not allowed to claim welfare benefits and must apply for support from the National Asylum Support Service (NASS). To qualify for NASS support asylum-seekers have to show they are destitute – i.e. little or no other means of support. NASS support for adults is about 30% less than the level of income support. Separated asylum-seeking children are supported by social services departments, under the Children Act 1989.

A joint study by Oxfam and the Refugee Council (2002), collecting evidence from 40 organisations, showed that asylum-seekers are forced to live at an unacceptable level of poverty. The study revealed that:

- 85 per cent of organisations reported that their clients experience hunger
- 95 per cent of organisations reported that their clients cannot afford to buy clothes or shoes
- 80 per cent of organisations reported that their clients are not able to maintain good health.

Asylum-seekers who have received positive decisions on their claim (Refugee Status, Exceptional Leave to Remain, Humanitarian Protection or Discretionary Leave) are eligible for welfare benefits, although they may continue to experience financial difficulties.

Main difficulties

Withdrawal of support from some asylum applicants

The government is able to deny some asylum-seekers access to NASS support if they did not apply for asylum 'as soon as reasonably practicable' or if they are unable to provide a clear and coherent account of how they came to the UK or accurate information about their circumstances. However asylum applicants should get NASS support whenever they apply for asylum if they have dependant children under 18, or special needs (e.g. disability). Unaccompanied asylum-seeking children are also not affected by this rule as they receive support from Social Services.

Poverty

New asylum-seekers are no longer allowed to work, and most are outside the benefits system. Income Support is usually the gateway to other payments and benefits, all of which are designed to help poor people meet additional essential costs. Most asylum-seekers are not entitled to claim any of these additional benefits, which include help for families with children, the elderly, people with disabilities, and pregnant and nursing mothers.

Negotiating bureaucracy

Understanding how the system works, being able to read official letters or fill in complex forms can be stressful and difficult for many parents.

Household services and utilities

Refugees are currently being dispersed around the country to areas that are unused to receiving them. This means they will be isolated from their support networks and may need help in learning about everyday living in the UK, including how to make things work, paying bills and where to find help when things go wrong. Common advice

needs include: heating; gas, electricity and water; TV licences; building maintenance.

Bank accounts

Asylum-seekers may experience difficulties in opening a bank account. The Co-operative Bank has been sympathetic to asylum-seekers in this situation (www.co-operativebank.co.uk).

Free school meals

Asylum-seeking and refugee families are entitled to free school meals if they receive a type of financial support that confers entitlement. Families will need to show some form of proof of the support they are receiving when they apply. See the DfES website for advice on entitlement to free school meals: www.parentcentre.gov.uk

Entitlement to free school meals

Children whose parents receive one or more of the following benefits or types of support are entitled to free school meals:

- Income Support (IS)
- Income-based Jobseeker's Allowance (IBJSA)
- support from NASS or a local authority asylum team
- Child Tax Credit, providing they are not entitled to Working Tax Credit and their annual income (as assessed by the Inland Revenue) does not exceed £13,910.

Changes of circumstance

Any means-tested benefits or asylum support that a family receives are liable to be reassessed (backdated, raised, reduced or even cut completely) if there has been a significant change of circumstances – eg, any change in family structure or change of address. Families should inform whatever organisation is providing the family with support (eg, the benefits office, local authority or NASS) immediately of any changes.

Debt

An inadequate income may mean that some families get into debt, often to their families and friends. Other families may already have significant debts if they were forced to borrow money to pay for their journey to safety. Some refugees and asylum-seekers may also get into debt due to applications for asylum support and benefits not being processed efficiently.

Good practice in school

Problems with benefits and money can be complex. In most cases, a parent will need specialised advice. Awareness of sources of local advice will assist schools in signposting parents to sources of help. Schools should be aware that

some groups might need advice and information that meet religious and cultural needs. For example, Muslim refugees may wish to access savings schemes that do not carry interest.

How schools can help with financial needs – a checklist

✓ Provide information on local advice services.
✓ Develop links with local advice services so that referrals can be made when needed.
✓ Help families apply for grants for essential items. The Family Welfare Association often provides help, and will accept referral letters from schools.
✓ Ensure that children access entitlement to free school meals.
✓ Help families understand letters they receive about benefits and other money matters.
✓ Provide letters of support – eg, for opening a bank account.
✓ Ensure that parents are aware they can ask for interpreters when dealing with NASS, the Department for Work and Pensions and utility suppliers.

Case study

A mother of two children about to start at the school applied for Income Support at Salusbury WORLD with the aid of an outreach worker from the local citizens advice bureau. The application was successful, but after four months of weekly payments, a two-week period passed during which the mother received no money. By the third week, payments had started again but the mother had

been left temporarily unable to support herself and her family. She came to Salusbury WORLD for help.

Salusbury WORLD contacted the Department for Work and Pensions with supportive evidence and it was discovered that an administrative error had occurred. Replacement cheques were to be sent and the school office agreed to provide free school meals for both children during the waiting period.

Further information and resources

Resources to help schools support parents

Parentaid
www.continyou.org.uk

Unit C1
Grovelands Court
Grovelands Estate
Longford Road
Exghall
Coventry CV7 9NE
Tel: 024 7658 8440
Email: info@continyou.org.uk

Continyou
17 Old Ford Road
London E2 0PJ
Tel: 020 8709 9900
Email: info@continyou.org.uk

Parentaid is both a process and a product. The process involves schools and other institutions which work with children in first identifying the concerns and problems about which parents are seeking support and advice, and then undertaking an audit of services within the local community which can provide that help. It helps those responsible for developing support services to identify gaps in existing provision.

The product resulting from this process is a customised directory of easily accessible information on local sources of support which professionals and volunteers can use to signpost parents to the advice and help they need.

Parentaid currently receives funding from the Family Support Unit of the Home Office.

ContinYou (formerly CEDC) can provide advice and support in setting up Parentaid Partnerships, and publishes *Parentaid: A 'how to' guide*.

General advice for refugees

The Refugee Council
www.refugeecouncil.org.uk
3 Bondway
London SW8 1SJ
Tel: 020 7820 3000

The Refugee Council is the largest organisation in the UK working with asylum-seekers and refugees. It provides direct advice to refugees and publishes translated information booklets. The Refugee Council has recently published *RADAR – Refugee Resources in the UK 2003*, a national CD-ROM directory with information on over 1,100 organisations providing services for asylum-seekers and refugees across the UK.

Refugee Council One Stop Service
240–250 Ferndale Road
London SW9 8DB
Tel: 020 7346 6700

Refugee Council Advice Line
Tel: 020 7346 6777
Mondays, Tuesdays, Thursdays and Fridays
10am–1pm, 2pm–5pm
Refugee Council regional offices:
West Midlands (Birmingham)
Tel: 0121 622 1515
Eastern Region (Ipswich) Tel: 01473 297900
Yorkshire and Humberside (Leeds)
Tel: 0113 244 9404

Refugee Action
www.refugee-action.org.uk
The Old Fire Station
150 Waterloo Road
London
SE1 8SB
Tel: 020 7654 7700

Refugee Action is an independent national charity that enables refugees to build new lives in the UK. It provides practical advice and assistance for newly arrived asylum-seekers and long-term commitment to their settlement through community development work.

Refugee Action regional offices:

Birmingham	Tel: 0121 693 9989
Bristol	Tel: 0117 989 2100
Leicester	Tel: 0116 261 4830
Leeds	Tel: 0113 244 5345
Liverpool	Tel: 0151 702 6300
Manchester	Tel: 0161 233 1200
Nottingham	Tel: 0115 941 8552
Plymouth	Tel: 01752 519860
Southampton	Tel: 023 8024 8130
Stockwell	Tel: 020 7735 5361

Refugee Arrivals Project
www.refugee-arrivals.org.uk
41b Cross Lances Road
Hounslow
Middlesex TW3 0ES
Tel: 020 8607 6888

The Refugee Arrivals Project provides assistance to new applicant asylum-seekers. It is the only voluntary organisation working with asylum-seekers directly after they arrive at airports in the south-east of England.

Migrant Helpline
www.migranthelpline.org.uk
The Rendezvous Building
Freight Service Approach Road
Eastern Docks
Dover CT16 1JA
Tel: 01304 203977

Migrant Helpline is an independent NGO providing a reception and advice service for newly arrived asylum-seekers and advice and support to refugees living in Kent and Sussex.

North of England Refugee Service
www.refugee.org.uk
2 Jesmond Road West
Newcastle upon Tyne NE2 4PQ
Tel: 0191 245 7311

The North of England Refugee Service is an independent organisation providing advice and support to asylum-seekers and refugees who have arrived or settled in the north of England.

Other North of England Refugee Service offices:
Newcastle   Tel: 0191 222 0406
Wallsend   Tel: 0191 200 1199
Sunderland   Tel: 0191 510 8685
Middlesborough Tel: 01642 217447

Scottish Refugee Council
www.scottishrefugeecouncil.org.uk
5 Cadogan Square
(170 Blythswood Court)
Glasgow G2 7PH
Tel: 0141 248 9799
Freephone number for newly-arrived and dispersed asylum-seekers: 0800 085 6087

The Scottish Refugee Council provides advice, information and assistance to asylum-seekers and refugees in Scotland.

Welsh Refugee Council
Cardiff   Tel: 02920 489800
Swansea   Tel: 01792 301729
Newport   Tel: 01633 266420
Wrexham   Tel: 01978 363240

Northern Ireland Council for Ethnic Minorities (NICEM)
www.nicem.org.uk
3rd Floor
Ascot House
24–31 Shaftesbury Square
Belfast BT2 7DB
Tel: 028 9023 8645

NICEM provides advice and support to destitute asylum-seekers. It also provides integration and resettlement support to refugees and people granted Humanitarian Protection and Discretionary Leave.

Citizens Advice Bureau (CAB)
www.citizensadvice.org.uk

The Citizens Advice Bureau Service offers free, confidential, impartial and independent advice. Citizens Advice Bureaux can help solve many problems including debt and consumer issues, benefits, housing, legal matters, employment, and immigration. Advisers can help fill out forms, write letters, negotiate with creditors and represent clients at court or tribunal.

Many CABs provide specialist advice, often in partnership with other agencies such as solicitors and the probation service. Local CABs often have advisers who specialise in refugee issues.

The CAB website has a Directory Search that provides information about local services.

AdviceUK
www.adviceuk.org.uk

AdviceUK is the UK's largest support network for free independent advice centres.

Citizens Advice Line for London (CALL)
www.cabline.org.uk

CALL operates a contact centre service, offering advice and information by telephone, email, fax and letter to people who live and/or work in London. CALL currently offers consumer, employment advice and housing advice.

Central London Advice Service (CLAS)
www.clas.org.uk

CLAS provides a free and confidential advice service as well as specialised money and debt advice, legal advice and advice for refugees and asylum-seekers.

British Red Cross
www.redcross.org.uk
International Welfare Service
44 Moorfields
London EC2Y 9AL
Tel: 020 7235 5454

The Red Cross International Tracing and Message Service helps families separated by armed conflict, political conflict or natural disaster to stay in contact. The service is free and confidential.

Refugee community organisations
There are refugee community organisations all over the UK. Many are well established and provide valuable support to their communities. Services provided will vary depending on the organisation's funding and resources. Many refugee community organisations provide advice and outreach support and have a detailed understanding of the needs of their community. The Refugee Council can provide information on local organisations. Other organisations that support the development of refugee community organisations include:

Evelyn Oldfield Unit
www.evelynoldfield.co.uk

The Evelyn Oldfield Unit provides specialist support and training for refugee organisations.

Praxis
www.praxis.org.uk
Pott Street
London E2 0EF
Tel: 020 7749 7600

The Praxis Community Participation Programme
supports member groups through leadership
development, capacity building, awareness-raising,
self-help initiatives, cultural affirmation and self-
advocacy. The Community Services Programme
provides specialist advice and support tailored to
the needs of refugee communities.

Redbridge Refugee Forum
www.refugeeforum.org
1st Floor
Broadway Chambers
1 Cranbrook Road
Ilford
Essex IG1 4DU
Tel: 020 8478 4513

Provides refugee community groups across east
London with community development support.

Legal advice and representation for refugees

The Refugee Legal Centre (RLC)
www.refugee-legal-centre.org.uk
153–157 Commercial Road
London E1 2DA
Tel: 020 7780 3200

The RLC provides legal advice and representation for those seeking protection under international and national human rights asylum law. Appointments and advice line: 020 7780 3220. The line is open from 9.30am to 1.00pm every weekday except Thursday.

Asylum Aid
www.asylumaid.org.uk
28 Commercial Street
London
E1 6LS
Tel: 020 7377 5123

Asylum Aid is a charity that provides free legal advice to refugees and asylum-seekers.
Advice line: 020 7377 5123.

Immigration Advisory Service (IAS)
www.iasuk.org
County House
190 Great Dover Street
London SE1 4XB
Tel: 020 7967 1200

The IAS gives free and confidential legal advice. It has offices all over the UK.

Telephone advice: 020 7967 1200 between 10am and 12.30pm on working days.

Telephone numbers for IAS regional offices are:

Birmingham	0121 616 3540
Cardiff	02920 496 662
Derby	01332 371 385
Glasgow	0141 248 2956
Hounslow	020 8607 6570 /
	020 8814 1115
Leeds	0113 244 2460
Leicester	0116 262 9899
Liverpool	0151 242 0920
Manchester	0161 834 9942
Middlesborough	01641 219222
Norwich	01603 496 623
Cambridgeshire	01954 783 333
Peterborough	01733 555 317

Joint Council for the Welfare of Immigrants (JCWI)
www.jcwi.org.uk
115 Old Street
London EC1V 9JR
Tel: 020 7251 8708

JCWI is an independent, national voluntary organisation campaigning for justice and combating racism in immigration and asylum law and policy. JCWI provides free advice and representation.

JCWI does not provide a drop-in advice service. All advice is available by telephone only.

Advice line: 020 7251 8706, Monday–Friday 10am–1pm.

Bail for Immigration Detainees (BID)
www.biduk.org
Tel: 020 7247 3590 (1.30pm–4.30pm Monday
to Friday)

BID provides a free, dedicated bail service for
those detained under immigration legislation.
BID does not deal with any other aspect of the
asylum process and does not offer legal advice on
general asylum matters.

**Immigration Law Practitioners Association
(ILPA)**
www.ilpa.org.uk
Lindsey House
40–42 Charterhouse Street
London EC1M 6JN
Tel: 020 7251 8383

ILPA is an association of lawyers specialising in
immigration law. It may be able to advise about
finding a solicitor.

Law centres
www.lawcentres.org.uk
Tel: 020 7387 8570

Law centres provide a free and independent
professional legal service for people who live or
work in their catchment areas. Law centres work
closely with their communities and provide the
kind of services that are most suitable for that
area. Telephone and drop-in advice is often
available.

Community Legal Service (CLS)
www.clsdirect.org.uk/index.jsp

This website enables you to search for legal
information and advice and locate an advice
provider in your area.

**The Office of the Immigration Services
Commissioner (OISC)**
www.oisc.co.uk
5th Floor, Counting House
53 Tooley Street
London SE1 2QN
Tel: 020 7211 1500

The OISC is an independent public body
responsible for ensuring that all immigration
advisers fulfil the requirements of good practice.
The OISC are committed to the elimination of
unscrupulous advisers and the fair and thorough
investigation of complaints. The OISC website
includes an 'Adviser Finder' section.

Solicitors and legal representatives
Most refugees have a solicitor or legal
representative advising them with their asylum
claim. Many firms of solicitors have specialist staff
working on immigration and asylum matters.
They may also have specialists in other areas of
law. Law centres, Citizens Advice Bureaux and the
Community Legal Service can help refugees find
legal advice.

Advice for young refugees, including separated and unaccompanied asylum-seekers

Refugee Council Children's Panel of Advisers for Unaccompanied Asylum-Seeking Children

The Home Office funds the panel to provide independent guidance and support to ensure that the child is aware of his or her rights and the services to which he or she is entitled.

Duty telephone: 020 7582 4947

Get Connected
www.getconnected.org.uk
Tel: 0808 808 4994

Get Connected is a UK-wide helpline for young people that finds the best help whatever the problem. The helpline workers listen to a young person, talk through the options, and make suggestions of where to get the best help. Get Connected then provides a free connection to the service chosen and can also text important information to mobile phones.

Open everyday from 1.00pm to 11.00pm.
Free calls from all landlines and mobile phones.

National Youth Advocacy Service (NYAS)
www.nyas.net
Freephone: 0800 616101

NYAS is a children's charity that offers socio-legal advocacy services to children, young people, parents, carers and professionals. NYAS provides independent representation and advice, ensuring that the voice of children and young people is heard in all matters affecting them. NYAS has advocates in most parts of England and Wales. If a problem can't be sorted out on the freephone helpline they can arrange a meeting with an advocate.

NYAS has recently started a legal service specifically for unaccompanied children who are seeking asylum.

ChildLine
www.childline.org.uk
Tel: 0800 1111

ChildLine is a free 24-hour helpline for children and young people in the UK. Advice is available on a wide range or problems including bullying, homelessness, racism and children's rights.

Kidscape
www.kidscape.org.uk

Kidscape is a national charity dedicated to preventing bullying and child sexual abuse. Kidscape offers advice to children and young people who are experiencing bullying, and an Anti-Bullying Helpline for parents/carers and concerned adults who need advice.

Kidscape Anti-Bullying Helpline: 08451 205 204.

Young separated refugees – a series of short guides
Published by Save the Children between September 2002 and May 2003. The guides are on:
- Rights and entitlements of separated refugee children
- Setting up mentoring schemes for young refugees
- Providing emotional support to young separated refugees
- Setting up youth groups for young refugees.

Free. To order copies contact Chris MacArthur on 020 8741 4054 ext. 101. Email: c.macarthur@scfuk.org.uk

Advice for refugee women

Refugee Women's Resource Project (RWRP)
www.asylumaid.org.uk/RWRP/RWRP.htm
Asylum Aid
28 Commercial Street
London E1 6LS
Tel: 020 7377 5123

The RWRP provides free legal representation and advice to women refugees and asylum-seekers.

Refugee Women's Association
www.refugeewomen.org.uk
Print House
18 Ashwin Street
London E8 3DL
Tel: 020 7923 2412

The Refugee Women's Association provides advice and guidance to refugee women on education, training, employment, health and social care. Support is provided at RWA's offices and on an outreach basis.

African Refugee Women's Access to Education and Training Project
www.aet.refugeewomen.care4free.net

The African Refugee Women's Access to Education and Training Project provides free educational and vocational training and advice for unemployed African women refugees and asylum-seekers. The project provides advice on how the new Immigration and Asylum Act affects refugees and asylum-seekers in the UK, particularly the changes in education and training entitlements.

It also assists refugee and women's groups throughout the UK to establish their own database of education and training opportunities.

The project has an information database with details of courses and programmes in the London area which offer special incentives for women. The courses and programmes provide funding or facilities for disability, childminding, nursery, crèche and travel costs which could specifically help refugee women.

Women's Aid
www.womensaid.org.uk

Women's Aid is the key national charity in England for women suffering physical, mental and/or sexual abuse by someone with whom she is or has been in a relationship.

Women's Aid National Domestic Violence Helpline: 0808 2000 247

Scottish Women's Aid
www.scottishwomensaid.co.uk

The website contains details of local support and advice across Scotland.

Welsh Women's Aid
www.welshwomensaid.org
Helpline: 0808 8010 800

Northern Ireland Women's Aid Federation
www.niwaf.org

NIWAF provides refugee and emotional support to women and their dependent children suffering from domestic abuse in the home.

Refuge 24-hour Domestic Violence Helpline:
Tel: 0870 599 5443

National crisis line, 24 hours a day, 365 days a year which provides advice and support to those experiencing domestic violence. Refers women and children to refuges nationwide.

Relate
www.relate.org.uk

Relate is the UK's largest relationship counselling organisation. Relate also offers individual counselling for young people aged 10–18 whose parents or carers are in conflict, going through a separation process or already separated. Young people can refer themselves for this service.

Couple Counselling Scotland
www.couplecounselling.org

Couple Counselling promotes, develops and co-ordinates a confidential counselling service for people in marriages and other intimate personal relationships.

Muslim Women's Help Line
www.mwhl.org
Tel: 020 8904 8193 or 020 8908 6715

Provides a free confidential listening service for Muslim women and girls.

Housing advice

Local authorities are responsible for ensuring that anyone in their district, including refugees and asylum-seekers, can get free housing advice if they are facing homelessness or bad housing conditions. This may be through their own housing advice or housing aid centres or from other advice or help centres. Contact the housing department to find out how to get housing advice in their area.

Shelter
www.shelter.org.uk
88 Old Street
London EC1V 9HU
Housing advice line: 0808 800 4444 (Free telephone call to Shelterline 24 hours)

This service provides basic information on rights and can also make a referral to local housing aid centres. If necessary it can also provide telephone interpretation for the call.

The Shelter website has details of all Shelter's local independent housing advice centres.

Shelter also runs the **National Homelessness Advice Service** (www.nhas.org.uk), a partnership with other frontline advice services which seeks to prevent and alleviate homelessness and housing problems by enabling the widest possible access to expert housing advice, information and advocacy. This can be accessed via **Citizens Advice Bureaux**, or in London via other advice agencies as well.

Housing Justice
www.justhousing.org.uk
209 Old Marylebone Road
London NW1 5QT
Tel: 020 7723 7273

Housing Justice is the national voice of Christian action in the field of housing.

Homeless Pages
www.homelesspages.org.uk

A web-based resource that provides information about homelessness, services for homeless people, training courses, publications, etc. A good one-stop information service.

Refugee Housing Association
www.refugeehousing.org.uk

The Refugee Housing Association (RHA) is one of the country's leading providers of housing and support to refugees and asylum-seekers. Most of their housing is filled by people nominated by local authorities or other services, so they cannot usually offer housing to anyone who applies directly.

Sue Lukes
www.sue.lukes.btinternet.co.uk.

The website of Sue Lukes, a consultant and adviser on refugees and housing. The site is useful for its regular information updates and details of training courses.

Health advice

National Health Service
www.nhs.uk

On the NHS website you can search for local GP services.

NHS Direct
www.nhsdirect.nhs.uk
Tel: 0845 4647

NHS Direct operates a 24-hour nurse advice and health information service, providing confidential information on:
- what to do if you or your family are feeling ill
- particular health conditions
- local healthcare services, such as doctors, dentists or late-night opening pharmacies
- self-help and support organisations.

The telephone service is available in England and Wales and a similar service, called NHS24, is available in Scotland. Tel: 08454 242424.

NHS Direct Confidential Translation Service
NHS Direct can provide confidential interpreters, in many languages, within minutes of your call. All you need to do is state in English the language you would prefer to use.

Ring the NHS Direct telephone number 0845 4647.

Health for Asylum-seekers and Refugees Portal (HARP)
www.harpweb.org.uk

HARP is a directory of information and resources concerning the health needs of asylum-seekers and refugees.

HARP Mental Health and Well-Being Web Resource
www.mentalhealth.harpweb.org.uk

A website designed to help health professionals assist asylum-seekers and refugees with mental health needs.

The Medical Foundation for the Care of Victims of Torture
www.torturecare.org.uk
111 Isledon Road,
London N7 7JW
Tel: 020 7697 7777

Medical Foundation Northwest Office
The Angel
St Philips Place (Off Chapel Street)
Salford M3 6FA
Tel: 0161 839 8090

The Medical Foundation provides medical treatment and therapeutic support to survivors of torture.

Minority Ethnic Health Inclusion Project (MEHIP)
Springwell House
Ardmillan Terrace
Edinburgh EH11 2JL
Tel: 0131 537 7576

MEHIP links minority ethnic individuals and communities with health services, to improve the accessibility and appropriateness of services across Lothian, Scotland.

Foundation for Women's Research and Development (FORWARD)
www.forwarduk.org.uk
Unit 4
765–767 Harrow Road
London NW10 5NY
Tel: 020 8960 4000

FORWARD is a non-governmental organisation promoting the health and human rights of African women and girls in the UK and Africa. FORWARD focuses on the elimination of harmful traditional practices such as female genital mutilation (FGM) by providing education and activities for community-based groups. The FORWARD website provides information of local specialist clinics.

Women's Health London
www.womenshealthlondon.org.uk
52 Featherstone Street
London EC1Y 8RT
Tel: 020 7251 6333

Women's Health provides health information on gynaecological health issues such as heavy bleeding, fibroids, hysterectomy, the menopause and HRT, pelvic inflammatory disease and ovarian problems.

MEDACT
www.medact.org

Medact is a health professional's organisation challenging barriers to health. Medact's website has information and links on refugee health issues.

Young Minds
www.youngminds.org.uk

Young Minds is a national charity committed to improving the mental health of all children and young people.

Department of Health mental health directory
www.doh.gov.uk

A nationwide directory of mental health organisations and information.

Meeting the Health Needs of Refugees and Asylum-seekers in the UK: An information and resource pack for health workers (2002)
www.london.nhs.uk/newsmedia/publications/Asylum_Refugee.pdf
by Angela Burnett and Yohannes Fassil
NHS/Department of Health

A comprehensive and clearly presented information and resource pack. Building on the skills and experience of health workers, the pack contains practical information, details of useful contacts and resources and includes examples of good practice from around the United Kingdom.

Further information and resources

Education, training and employment advice

Refugee Education and Training Advisory Service/Education Action International (EAI)
www.education-action.org
14 Dufferin Street,
London EC1Y 8PD
Tel. 020 7426 5800
Advice Line: 020 7426 5801

Refugee Education Training Advice Service (RETAS), a division of Education Action International, provides information, advice and guidance on education, training and employment for refugees. The service is free of charge, strictly confidential, and available to all adult (16+) asylum-seekers and refugees. EAI advisors provide in-depth interviews, assess prior qualifications, skills and experience, and give information on courses in adult, further and higher education as well as career and employment opportunities. Support is also available with CV writing, completing job applications and starting up your own business

The Refugee Council Training and Employment Section
www.refugeecouncil.org.uk
164 Clapham Park Road
London SW4 7DE
Tel: 020 7501 0990
Advice Line: 020 7346 6760

The Refugee Council Training and Employment Section gives advice on education, training and employment and runs a range of courses for refugees. It provides one-to-one interviews with qualified vocational advice workers who provide information and guidance on education and training courses in the UK, career development, professional re-qualification for those with overseas qualifications and making applications for financial help (for training and education). It also provides work experience placements, job search support, information on job vacancies, access to stationary, stamps, photocopier, telephone and fax, and free Internet access.

Refugee Assessment and Guidance Unit (RAGU)
www.unl.ac.uk/ragu
The Learning Centre University of North London
236–250 Holloway Road
London N7 6PP
Tel: 020 7753 5044

RAGU was set up to improve the employment prospects of refugees and asylum-seekers with higher-level education or professional qualifications from their own countries. RAGU offer various services including specifically targeted courses, individual advice and guidance sessions, and help into employment through the SET UP project. The aim is to enhance students' language skills, build self-confidence and open up possible avenues into education, vocational training and employment.

RAGU has a team of advisers who offer advice and guidance on routes to higher education, re-qualification in the UK, funding availability for higher education and Accreditation of Prior Experiential Learning (APEL).

RAGU and the DfES have also developed a new University Certificate in Educational Partnership Programme. This is a course for refugees, asylum-seekers and others who would like to work in schools, supporting refugee children and their families and advocating on their behalf. The course includes a placement in a school included in the programme.

Refugees into Jobs

3–7 Carlton Avenue (East)
Off Preston Road
Wembley
Middlesex HA9 8UA
Tel: 020 8908 4433

Refugees into Jobs helps refugees and asylum-seekers living in Brent and Harrow into jobs. It provides training, assistance with job search, voluntary work experience placements, and support with travelling and childcare.

UK National Academic Recognition Information Centre (UK NARIC)

www.naric.org.uk
ECCTIS 2000 Ltd.
Oriel House
Oriel Road
Cheltenham GL50 1XP
Tel: 01242 260010

The National Academic Recognition Information Centre for the United Kingdom (UK NARIC) advises on how overseas academic qualifications relate to UK qualifications. The service covers a wide range of countries, and staff can advise on the standing of international qualifications with UK professional bodies.

Council for Assisting Refugee Academics (CARA)

www.academic-refugees.org

CARA assists university teachers or researchers who have lost their jobs as a result of political, racial or religious discrimination and have become refugees in this country.

Africa Educational Trust (AET)

www.africaeducationaltrust.mcmail.com
38 King Street
London WC2 8JR
Tel: 020 7836 5075

The AET supports education for students from any part of Africa, but its major interest has always been to help people from areas where there is civil war or conflict. For many years the main focus of its work was on providing study grants and scholarships for South Africans and Namibians who had suffered from apartheid. During the late 1980s and early 1990s the Trust also supported a large programme of grants and scholarships for refugees in Britain, particularly for students from Ethiopia, Eritrea, Somalia and Sudan.

Praxis

www.praxis.org.uk
Pott Street
London E2 0EF
Tel: 020 7749 7600

Provides advice on education in the UK for refugees, and also runs vocational training courses.

Educational Grants Advisory Service (EGAS)

www.egas-online.org.uk

EGAS provides advice and guidance to enable students – or would-be students – to secure funding for post-16 education and training. The service operates nationally and offers comprehensive advice and information on statutory and non-statutory sources of funding.

153

Priority is given to people with special difficulties, including low-income groups, lone parents, people with disabilities and refugees.

Ruth Hayman Trust
www.ruthhaymantrust.com

The Ruth Hayman Trust gives small personal grants to support the education and training of adults who live in the UK and speak English as a second or other language. For example, help with examination and tuition costs or to buy books and equipment.

National Association for Teaching English and other Community Languages to Adults (NATECLA)
www.natecla.org.uk

NATECLA's aim is to provide a national forum for ESOL and community languages, to offer support and training, and to campaign on educational issues.

The National Institute of Adult Continuing Education (NIACE)
www.niace.org.uk

NIACE works to widen access to learning opportunities and increase participation among those groups currently under-represented in education and training.

Learning and Skills Council
www.lsc.gov.uk

The Learning and Skills Council is responsible for funding and planning education and training for over 16-year-olds in England. Their work covers further education, work-based training and young people, workforce development, adult and community learning, information, advice and guidance for adults and education business links.

Basic Skills Agency
www.basic-skills.co.uk

The Basic Skills Agency is the national agency for basic skills in England and Wales and is supported and funded by the government.

Education UK
www.educationuk.org

The Education UK website helps international students interested in studying for a UK course or qualification.

Learndirect
www.learndirect.co.uk

Learndirect offers a range of flexible courses to help people learn about computers, office skills and self-development. Learndirect courses are primarily online, enabling people to work at their own pace from home, at work or in a Learndirect centre.

The website has a database of 500,000 courses nationwide as well as practical information and advice on learning.

Scholarship Search UK
www.scholarship-search.org.uk

Scholarship Search UK provides a free database of undergraduate and postgraduate awards, and many other forms of student funding including commercial sponsorship, competitions and prizes, expedition awards and help with childcare costs.

Money and benefits advice

Citizens Advice Bureaux
www.citizensadvice.org.uk

Citizens Advice Bureaux give free, confidential, impartial and independent advice on a range of subjects, including money and benefits. Visit the website to find your nearest CAB.

Child Poverty Action Group
www.cpag.org.uk
94 White Lion Street
London N1 9PF
Tel: 020 7837 7979

CPAG promotes action for the relief, directly or indirectly, of poverty among children and families with children. It works to ensure that those on low incomes get their full entitlement to welfare benefits. CPAG publishes the *Welfare Benefits & Tax Credits Handbook 2003/2004.*

London Advice Service Alliance (LASA)
www.lasa.org.uk
Universal House
88–94 Wentworth Street
London E1 7SA
Tel: 020 7377 2748
Benefits Advice Line: 020 7247 1735 (Tuesday, Wednesdays and Fridays between 10.30am and 12.30pm).

The LASA advice line provides welfare benefits information to advisers within the Greater London area.

Rightsnet
www.rightsnet.org.uk

LASA's Rightsnet website provides support and information about welfare rights for advice workers.

Multikulti
www.multikulti.org.uk

The Multikulti website aims to support citizenship through the delivery of culturally appropriate and accurately translated information in the areas of welfare law, debt, employment, health, housing, immigration and welfare benefits.

The Family Welfare Association (FWA)
www.fwa.org.uk
501–505 Kingsland Road
London E8 4AU
Tel: 020 7254 6251

The Family Welfare Association is a national organisation (England only) offering advice, grants and support to children and families in need. In 2002, the FWA distributed over £1 million in small grants to provide basic needs such as bedding, children's clothing or a cooker.

Prisoners of Conscience
www.prisonersofconscience.org

Prisoners of Conscience helps those who have been persecuted for their political or religious beliefs or ethnic origin, providing they have not used or advocated violence. The organisation's central aim is to raise and distribute money to help prisoners of conscience and/or their families rehabilitate themselves during and after their ordeal and offer short-term economic relief.

PO Box 36789
London SW9 9XF
Tel: 020 7738 7511

National Debtline
www.nationaldebtline.co.uk
Tel: 0808 808 4000

A helpline that provides free, confidential and independent advice on how to deal with debt problems.

Note

1 Asylum-seekers and refugees: education, training, employment, skills and services in Coventry and Warwickshire, University of Birmingham Centre for Urban and Regional Studies/NIACE (2003)

Local services information

Name of organisation:

Profile:

Address:

Contact details: Tel:

                           Fax:

                           Email:

                           Website:

Opening hours/contact times:

Contact person:

Services offered:

One-to-one support	Practical support
Group support	Advice/information
Outreach	Other
Interpreting	Gender/ethnic specific

Referral procedures:

Other information:

Adapted from: *Parentaid: A 'how to' guide*, CEDC (2003)

Bibliography

Burnett, A and Fassil, Y (2002) *Meeting the Health Needs of Refugees and Asylum-seekers in the UK: An information and resource pack for health workers*, NHS/Department of Health

ContinYou (1999) *Parentaid – school and community working together to support parents*

Department for Education and Skills (2003) *Aiming High: Raising the achievement of minority ethnic pupils*, Department for Education and Skills

Department of Health, the Home Office and the Department for Education and Skills (2003) *What to do if you're worried a child is being abused – Children's services guidance*

National Union of Teachers (2002) *Relearning to Learn: Advice to teachers new to teaching children from refugee and asylum-seeking families*, National Union of Teachers

Newham Education Action Zone (2003) *Managing Mid-phase Pupil Admissions: A resource and guidance folder for school*, Newham Education Action Zone

Ofsted (2000) *Evaluating Educational Inclusion*

Ofsted (2002) *Managing Pupil Mobility*

Ofsted (2003) *The Education of Asylum-seeker Pupils*

Oxfam and the Refugee Council (2002) *Poverty and Asylum in the UK*

Refugee Council *Words for School Use*

Richman, N (1998) *In the Midst of the Whirlwind: A manual for helping refugee children*, Trentham Books

Rutter, J (2003) *Working with Refugee Children*, Joseph Rowntree Foundation

Shelter (2001) *Far from Home*

Standards and Quality in Education 2001/02, Annual Report of Her Majesty's Chief Inspector of Schools, The Stationery Office

Stanley, K (2001) *Cold Comfort: Young separated refugees in England*, Save the Children

Stead, J (2003) *Parentaid: A 'how to' guide*, CEDC

UN Convention on the Status of Refugees, 1951